No............................... Class..............................

Author ....

Title..

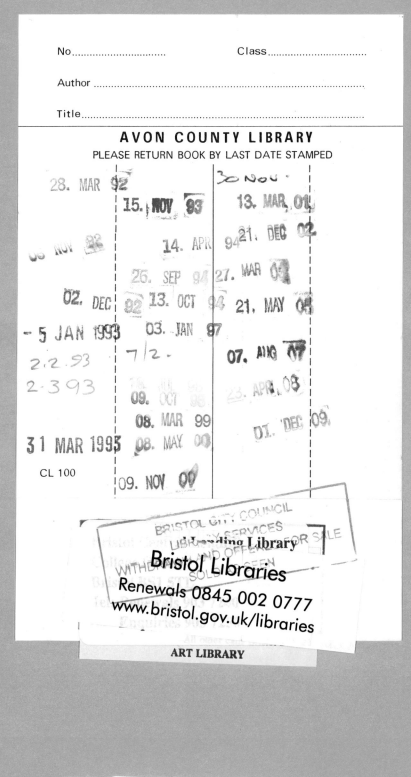

OUR VANISHING
HERITAGE

OUR VANISHING HERITAGE

MARCUS BINNEY

Arlington Books
King Street St. James's
London

OUR VANISHING HERITAGE
First published 1984 by
Arlington Books (Publishers) Ltd
15–17 King Street, St. James's
London SW1

© *Marcus Binney 1984*

Typeset by Inforum Ltd, Portsmouth
Colour separations by Fotographics
Printed and bound in England by
Hazell Watson & Viney Ltd, Aylesbury

British Library Cataloguing in Publication Data
Binney, Marcus
Our vanishing heritage.
1. Historic buildings—Great Britain—Conservation
and restoration
I. Title
363.6'9'0941   NA109.G7
ISBN 0-85140-635-1

PREVIOUS PAGE: Garden pavilion at Copped Hall near Epping, Essex. The house, gutted by fire in 1915, is now a shell. The Edwardian garden pavilions survive to testify to the splendour of the formal gardens.

CONTENTS

ACKNOWLEDGEMENTS

In the course of visiting the buildings and places described in this book, and in fighting to save many from demolition and to find new uses for them, I have received help, advice and information from numerous people, in particular colleagues at SAVE Britain's Heritage and *Country Life*. My thanks are due to the following: George Allan, Sara Alleyn, Colin Amery, Sophie Andreae, Clive Aslet, David Atwell, Lawrence Banks, Paul Barker, Oliver Barrett, Mavis Batey, Rodney Bellamey, Peter Burman, Donald Buttress, Tony Byrne, Timothy Cantell, Hugh Cantile, David Cooper, John Cornforth, Robert Cornwath, Alan Crawford, Stephen Croad, Anne Crook, J. Mordaunt Crook, Christopher Dalton, Gillian Darley, Martin Drury, Mark Fiennes, Donald Findlay, Ron Fitzgerald, Adrian Fort, Jennifer Freeman, Jonathan Gibson, Michael Gillingham, Mark Girouard, Andor Gomme, Catherine Griffiths, Douglas Hague, Max Hanna, Richard Haslam, Georgina Harford, John and Eileen Harris, Celia de la Hey, Peter Hodson, Kay Hubble, Richard Hughes, Gervase Jackson Stops, Jennifer Jenkins, Simon Jenkins, Brian Lang, Alastair Laing, Calder Loth, Randolph Langenbach, David Lowenthal, Francis Machin, Kit and Sally Martin, Barry Mazur, Emma Milne, Christopher Monkhouse, Lord Montagu, Susan Moore, Jane Morton, Robin Ollington, Julian Orbach, Trevor Osborne, David Pearce, Michael Pearce, Ken and Sue Powell, Jane Preger, Kate Pugh, Hugh de Quetteville, John Redmill, Peter Reid, Anthony and Margaret Richardson, Martin Richardson, Tim Riviere, Piers Rodgers, Richard Rogers, Matthew Saunders, John Smith, Alex Starkey, Freddie Stockdale, Roy Strong, Reginald Thompson, Peter Thornton, Tony Venison, Robin Wade, David Walker, Roger White, Trevor Wood and finally my wife, Anne, for help and encouragement of every kind.

The suggestion for this book came initially from Christine Lunness of Arlington Books. I also owe my thanks to Desmond Elliott, publisher, and Deirdre, Diana, Margaret and Ondine at Arlington Books without whom this book would not have been published.

PICTURE ACKNOWLEDGEMENTS

Ian Beazley: 228; Marcus Binney: 19, 27, 35, 39, 50–51, 54B, 66, 95, 143A, 143B, 154, 183, 203, 207, 234A, 234B, 238, 251, 254A, 254B; Cambridge University Collection: 88, 92, 93; *Country Life*: 16, 22, 29, 94, 98, 100, 110–111, 114; *Country Life* photographs by Alex Starkey, 76, 78, 123; *Country Life* photographs by Paul G. Beswick, 118, 151A, 151B; *Country Life* photographs by Jonathan Gibson, 212, 244; Christopher Dalton, 2, 68, 70, 84, 102, 103, 113, 157, 217, 176; John Donat, 61; Department of the Environment: 57–57, 171, Mark Fiennes: 135, 179, 190, 195, 246; Greater London Council: 138; Randolph Langenbach: 208, 236; National Monuments Record: 12, 13, 24–25, 32, 36, 42, 45, 126, 163; National Trust Archive, Dublin: 202; Keith Parkinson: 174, 176, 184, 230; SAVE: 196; Times Newspapers Ltd: 192; Robin Wade: 10.

To Sarah, Matthew, Sophie, Catherine, Ken, Emma, Sara, Celia and Charlotte

INTRODUCTION

"WHY DON'T THE PRESERVATIONISTS put their money where their mouths are?" This angry challenge is made almost every time someone speaks up to save a fine building from destruction. The purpose of this book is to show there are good tough answers to such questions. Practical, and sympathetic, solutions can be found for the great majority of historic buildings if only those who decide their fate can be persuaded to give them a chance. All too often alternatives have not been seriously considered. The individual can stand up and fight the inertia and indifference of government departments, public authorities, nationalised industries, property developers and large urban landlords. He can interest owners and planners in solutions. He can win the support of councillors and MPs and break through the defensive lines of Whitehall and persuade Ministers to act.

One of the great freedoms in Britain is the right of free association and, as this book shows, endangered buildings have been reprieved and saved by quite small groups of people who have been able to win popular support for their cause. The National Trust now has more than a million members, but the Trust's energies are inevitably absorbed almost wholly in caring for its own superb properties which are preserved in perpetuity for the enjoyment of the public. Only a small proportion of the many beautiful buildings in Britain can become showplaces: the overwhelming majority, if they are to survive, must continue in use or if necessary find an alternative use.

This book describes buildings I have visited over the last fifteen years, but mostly over the last five. Many of these visits have been to

ABOVE: The Hall of Lost Houses at the exhibition *The Destruction of the Country House* held at the Victoria & Albert Museum in 1974.

places in danger, buildings threatened with demolition or simply left empty and decaying. This might sound a depressing quest and it would be if it was a hopeless one. In fact, it has led me to many stunningly beautiful and, often largely forgotten, places. The search for decaying buildings is almost always a journey of discovery. Faced with the challenge of finding new uses for these buildings, many of my journeys have been to buildings which have been successfully given a new lease of life, not just as expense of the taxpayer or ratepayer but often on a wholly commercial basis.

I began as an observer, rapidly became involved in working out solutions for decaying buildings and ultimately in setting up trusts to restore them. These journeys were first made while seeking material for articles in *Country Life* which I joined in 1968 as architectural writer. Other places I have visited while helping to prepare a series of exhibitions for Roy Strong at the Victoria and Albert

Museum (*The Destruction of the Country House* in 1974 with John Harris and Peter Thornton; *Change and Decay: The Future of our Churches* with Peter Burman in 1977, and a conservation section for the exhibition, *The Garden* which John Harris organised in 1979.)

I have travelled to see many threatened buildings as Chairman of SAVE Britain's Heritage, which I was involved in founding in 1975, European Architectural Heritage Year. Further material results from work on two reports published by the British Tourist Authority, *Chapels and Churches: Who Cares?* (*1977*), and that of the committee on alternative uses for historic buildings chaired by Lord Montagu, which appeared in 1980.

The common feature in all these journeys is that you never know when you set out what you will find on arrival. In many cases a building is familiar through photographs, its case history documented by correspondence but every time, invariably, surprise awaits. However parlous or problematic the state of the building, there is almost always something to give one heart: an unexpectedly striking or unspoilt setting, the quality of its design and construction. Some of the most bizarre of all the journeys have been not to the buildings, but to meetings to try and resolve their future.

The battles described in this book have, for the most part, been fought in public and constantly in the press. Hence the campaigns can be followed, and vividly documented, through newspapers reports, magazine articles and readers' letters, as well as correspondence with owners, planners and Ministers. The buildings described vary widely in date and type. Some are acknowledged masterpieces, others of local charm or significance. In case after case, they have been dismissed as "white elephants" or lost causes, but given a determined and imaginative approach, time after time, a practical solution for their preservation has emerged.

COUNTRY HOUSES

SIFTING THROUGH A PILE of old country house guides one rainy afternoon, I chanced on a plain-covered volume entitled *Unusable Houses and Antique Furniture*. I blinked. What could this mean? The curious title was explained further inside. "The Unusable House, being notes on the disposal of certain old houses and of antique furniture, with a few words on the importance of fire insurance." The book bore no date but the print and the contents suggested it dated from the 1930s. It had been compiled by a firm of auctioneers in Bridgnorth, Shropshire, Perry and Phillips Ltd. They claimed they were the "pioneers in the business of separately disposing the fixtures and fittings of houses which have been condemned as useless for further occupation". The book was intended for "those who find themselves burdened with unusable or unsaleable country residences" and forms a fascinating, if melancholy, parade of houses demolished or stripped of their contents in the 1920s and early 1930s, with occasional fleeting hints as to why they had become "white elephants".

The second page is boldly headed *Demolition Sales*. "Many cultured people," it begins, "are inclined to think that those who take a responsible part in the 'demolishing' of an old country mansion must necessarily be vandals. This is a harsh judgement, and one which is, in nearly all cases, unfounded. Practically none of the old houses which were illustrated here, and which have been demolished, were of sufficient artistic beauty, architectural interest

OPPOSITE: Nuthall Temple, Nottinghamshire, built in 1754, and demolished in 1929. Sumptuous rococo plasterwork by Thomas Wright.

or historical association to justify the expense of a continued existence; whilst in every case it was financially impracticable to remodel
the residence in accordance with modern ideas of hygiene and
comfort."

The houses illustrated in the pages which followed today seem
far from devoid of quality. Pride of place must go to Nuthall
Temple in Nottinghamshire, a wonderful Palladian villa which the
book acknowledges "contained some of the finest rococo plasterwork in England". Designed by the architect and astronomer,
Thomas Wright, in 1754, Nuthall was ignominiously demolished in
1929. Doors, we are told in a matter of fact way, "made up to £20
each. Mantlepieces £170. Four stone sphinxes were sold for £590.
The fabric was purchased for rebuilding purposes". What this
means is unclear – does Nuthall Temple languish in packing-cases in
some Los Angeles warehouse, or were the stones sold off for use on
new houses nearby?

A similar questionmark hangs over Drayton Manor in
Staffordshire which went in 1926. The cryptic entry runs: "Built by
the great Sir Robert Peel. Its size made it entirely unwieldy for
occupation as a residence. The Statesmens' Gallery, with its marble
pillars, was sold practically as a whole and removed for re-erection."

On the next page is a photograph of Normanton Hall, the great
Palladian seat of the Heathcote family in Rutland, demolished in
1924. "It possessed no lighting facilities," is the melancholy epitaph.
Glossop Hall in Derbyshire, seat of the Lord Howard of Glossop,
appeared luckier. "Catalogued in 800 losts for demolition, but
acquired by the Local Authorities for a Museum." But this was only
a temporary reprieve, for Glossop was demolished in 1957.

Of Streatham Castle in Durham, one of the great Baroque
houses of the north, which was demolished in 1933, we are told,
simply " . . . the oak-panelling in the various rooms realized high
prices." Yet not one photograph of these magnificent interiors is
known today.

A few pages later comes Sprotborough Hall near Doncaster, a
glorious house of the 1690s, demolished in 1926. "The fine Carolean
screen and several pine panelled rooms," we learn, "realized a
substantial total." Nor were more modern houses exempt. Richard
Norman Shaw's great house at Dawpool, Cheshire, built in 1882,

went little more than forty years later. The brief note runs, "Quite a modern house, built chiefly of red sandstone, with a minstrels' gallery. Italian stone and marble chimneypieces. Nearly all the fittings were used for interior work in other houses."

For most people the real revelation of the scale of losses of country houses came at the Victoria and Albert Museum exhibition *The Destruction of the Country House* in 1974. "I thought the exhibition was superb," one leading financer wrote to Roy Strong "but the hall of destruction was so painful I could not bear to remain there more than one minute." Robin Wade, the exhibition designer, had conceived the hall of destruction, the centrepiece of the exhibition, as a three dimensional realization of the frescoes in the famous giants room at the Palazzo del Te in Mantua, where the giants, in a vain attempt to reach Olympus, are crushed by falling rocks and pillars. The hall of destruction was lined on two sides by giant columns frozen in the moment of collapse, with blown up photographs of lost houses pasted round the column shafts. On the opposite walls were hundreds more photographs of lost houses laid row above row like brickwork. All this was accompanied by the doomladen voice of John Harris reciting the roll of the fallen houses, county by county, as if they were names on a war memorial, grouped by regiment.

The purpose of the exhibition was to create awareness, to show how much had gone, to demonstrate how immediate the danger was to those that remained. Among my tasks as one of the organisers, was to collect and present material on houses then in danger, and to suggest possible solutions. So began a long series of journeys to look at empty and decaying country houses, as well as to many others which have been adapted, with varying degrees of sympathy and success, to new uses.

Initially I imagined that many of these abandoned houses would be suffering from some overwhelming handicap which would make it inconceivable that anyone would want to live there. Osbert Lancaster in his *Scene Changes* (1978) set the scene in a series of cartoons drawn specially for the exhibition, recording how 'progress' had treated some of the great houses of English literature. Disraeli's house, Brentham was shown still requisitioned by the War Office, surrounded by barbed wire and broken statuary;

Thomas Love Peacock's Crotchet Castle had been taken over by the Pang Valley Grit and Gravel Company – and huge mounds of gravel obliterated the lawns; Dickens' Chesney Wold revealed a new motorway cut through the garden.

Fates such as these, I found, had indeed overtaken numerous houses. Yet the more houses I visited, the more I was amazed to find how often the setting was in fact unspoilt, and sometimes positively idyllic. Again and again it emerged that neither the building nor its condition nor the cost of repairing it was not the real problem. In many cases it was the attitude of the owner – and most of these problem owners had acquired the houses fairly recently. Even if they did not want the house, they were unwilling to sell it. Even if the house was for sale, the terms were often wholly unreasonable – the price was enormous, given the condition of the building. In some cases virtually no land – not even the original garden – was offered with the house.

This chapter looks at a series of long-standing cases, describing the bizarre entanglements in which such houses can be caught. However, even in the most extreme circumstances the situation is rarely beyond hope. The most derelict houses have been saved but the real battle has been to gain possession of them.

FINEDON HALL

Two of the most wretchedly neglected country houses I have seen lie within six or seven miles of each other on either side of Wellingborough in Northamptonshire. These are Finedon Hall described by Pevsner as a "Gothic-cum-Tudor fantasy of William Mackworth-Dolben", and Ecton Hall which Pevsner proclaims "the foremost example of the early Gothic Revival in the county".

An article on Finedon Hall in *Country Life* in 1901, just four years after the magazine was launched, concluded: "Northampton-shire has more famous houses, but few more satisfactory and none better cared for, than Finedon Hall." The illustrations show neat Victorian parterres, raised flowerbeds of amazing complexity, and

OPPOSITE ABOVE: Finedon Hall in Northamptonshire, about 1980.
BELOW: The formal gardens at Finedon in 1901.

17

heliotropes growing proudly above circles of bedding out plants. "The gardens and pleasure grounds," the author says, "are remarkably beautiful." He goes on to describe "a noble avenue of stately limes" leading up to the house, a fine arboretum and "a large sheet of water, which in the winter is the resort of large numbers of wildfowl." The finest feature was a magnificent triple avenue of limes and chestnuts, enclosed in an ancient holly hedge.

When I saw Finedon in the summer of 1982 it was a wreck, but still remarkably beguiling. Its appeal lay partly in the rich ochre of the local building stone, partly in the sheer playful extravagance of its architecture. William Mackworth-Dolben (1806–72) who built the house was evidently an impish figure and like Frank Crisp at Friar Park outside Henley, fond of architectural quirks, and with no shortage of money to indulge his tastes. He had added the name of Dolben to Mackworth after his marriage in 1835 to Frances, the granddaughter of the fourth baronet of Finedon Hall, Sir John English Dolben. Both Mackworths and Dolbens had Welsh blood and the gables of the entrance front were emblazoned with the words *Gwell Angau na Cywilydd* – Rather Death than Shame – the motto of the Welsh Guards and now an all too apt epitaph for the house itself.

The house stands on the edge of the small town of Finedon. Driving through the town, William Mackworth-Dolben's engaging eccentricity is apparent in almost every street: in the Bell Inn, the Almshouses and the Ice Tower and numerous curiously named cottages, Thingdon Cottage, Ice Brook Cottage and Windmill Cottage – the latter was an earlier building to which he added a battlemented top so that it looks like a castle on a chess board. Looking at the datestones on all these buildings, and on the house, it appears that Mackworth-Dolben was building continuously for nearly four decades, beginning in 1835.

The first sign of the Hall, approaching from the town, is the massive wall of the garden – complete with Gothic buttresses through which there is a glimpse of the Museum tower. Today this has a searing gash in one corner. The scale of the tower is astonishing

OPPOSITE: The entrance front at Finedon. Built of local ironstone, the house has a wealth of ornamental detail.

– like the centrepiece of a great Victorian school or hospital. Yet on entering the courtyard in which it stands one sees it is not part of the house itself, but in the corner of a superb court of battlemented stables and outbuildings which would stand well in Oxford or Cambridge. The house backs onto the courtyard but the two main fronts look out over the pleasure grounds which in summer are now almost choked with undergrowth.

Decay had set in in 1971 when Colonel Baranger, the last owner to live in the house, died. The next year house and contents were put up for sale and the wretched sight that greeted visitors is described in John Bailey's history of the house and village *Finedon otherwise Thindgon* (1975): "The exterior so badly in need of attention, the unspeakable piles of rubbish in the outbuildings, the utterly unkempt gardens and the interior exhibiting decay at every turning."

In 1982 the house was in an advanced state of collapse but not beyond salvation. Roofs were falling in, masonry had tumbled, ornamental detail had disappeared but most of the main external walls were intact. However, the nature of Finedon's tragedy became apparent on rounding the garden front. There, across the Victorian pleasure grounds, were rows and rows of neat and substantial new houses. Yet even so, Finedon retained sufficient garden and privacy to make conversion into houses and flats a possibility. Plans were obtained from Wellingborough District Council and with Kit Martin, an architect specialising in the rescuing of country houses, we worked out the elements of a scheme. The newly-formed Northamptonshire Buildings Preservation Trust adopted the idea but when the Historic Buildings Council refused a grant, it had to withdraw.

In October 1983 a public inquiry was held into a new application by the owners to demolish which Wellingborough District Council had reluctantly to decide it could no longer oppose. However, the planning history of the house is worth retelling as a cautionary tale of the way in which a fine house in reasonable condition can become a pawn in a battle to obtain permission to develop the grounds.

In September 1971 planning permission was granted to the executors of Colonel Baranger for a change of use to a residential country club. Five months later the Hall was acquired by St Clair

Wade Holdings Ltd who applied for permission to convert the house into an arts centre with, dread thought, "residential development of the grounds". The application was turned down following an inquiry but the inspector ironically opened the way for new applications. While agreeing with the council that the best planning objective was the preservation of Finedon Hall without a material change of use, he concluded: "This is unlikely to happen unless extensive and remunerative development is permitted". This was in 1974. Had all this been just six or eight years later there would have been no difficulty in demonstrating that the house itself could be divided internally as flats and houses without the need for development in the grounds.

Two months later the Hall was put up for auction by order of the Mortgagees and was unexpectedly bought back by St Clair Wade Holdings. The Borough Council then agreed to the use of the Hall as offices and for six residential plots, and later to "four new blocks of good quality flats" in the grounds. Permission was granted on condition the owners retained and restored the Hall and stables as part of the overall development. Yet the situation was such that in October 1975 the Council served an Urgent Repairs Notice on St Clair Wade Holdings, requiring boarding up of windows, spraying of infected woodwork, cleaning of gutters and replacement of slipped roof slates. During the winter the Council carried out the works itself. A further application in February 1976 to demolish the entire house and stables and build 70 houses nearby was refused. A new application in December to adapt the Hall as an antiques centre with three flats, to convert the stables into eight houses and build 25 houses in the grounds, was approved the next April. The Borough, determined to ensure the Hall was restored, required the owner to pay a deposit of thirty per cent of the proceeds of any sale of land or buildings to the Council which would be spent on repairs to the house and outbuildings.

In June 1978 the owner gave notice to the Council that a consultant engineer had advised that the tower was dangerous and it was proposed to start work on demolishing the top third. The Council's Chief Building Engineer examined the tower and concluded it was *not* in any imminent danger. Demolition nonetheless began. The Council served an enforcement notice declaring the

ABOVE & OPPOSITE: Finedon stable wing in 1900 and 1983. Demolition began on the majestic museum tower without consent.

removal of the pyramid roof and north gable illegal. The owner appealed. A public inquiry was held but the appeal was subsequently withdrawn. Meanwhile unauthorised demolition work on the tower had continued.

Further enforcement notices were served by the Council – Mr Wade of St Clair Wade Holdings appealed. Meanwhile the Council decided to investigate the possibility of a housing association taking on the Hall, only to be told in 1981 that the Department of the Environment would not approve the project. Other schemes have subsequently been investigated but all have come to nothing.

But Finedon Hall is not yet lost. Following a public inquiry in October 1983 the Secretary of State for the Environment refused permission to demolish. In his report the inspector at the inquiry stated: "Nobody questions the intrinsic architectural and historic interest of the building . . . Its merits not being in doubt it is necessary to consider the condition of the building and whether

every possible effort has been made to put it to some suitable use."
He recognized that Finedon Hall was in a deplorable state but
pointed out that no detailed proposals had been put forward for the
site if it was demolished. He felt the existing walls were sound
enough for considerable portions of the house to be incorporated in
new houses. He preferred this to the proposed use of salvaged
materials in replacement buildings. Although " . . . the applicant
company as presently constituted may not be responsible for dereliction which has occurred in the immediate past, the ownership of
the Hall, nevertheless, remains the same." So he concluded " . . . in
the absence of any well-defined advantages to be gained from its
demolition (except possibly to the owners) my own view is that
permission for demolition would be premature." Hope for Finedon
lives again.

ECTON

Finedon's twin is Ecton Hall. It also stands on the edge of a village, but this time a very pretty village hardly affected by new development. The house stands just beyond the church, in the position of a medieval manor.

Facing south with a marvellous view across a stretch of park to fields and to woods beyond, it is only a few miles from Northampton, and would readily find a buyer if only it was put up for sale with a reasonable area of grounds. The garden front is one of the most delightful pieces of eighteenth-century Gothic architecture to be found anywhere in England. The design is attributed to the gentleman-architect, Sanderson Miller (1716–80) whose ruined tower at Hagley in Worcestershire was commended by Horace Walpole as possessing "the true rust of the Barons' Wars". The front

BELOW: Ecton House, Northamptonshire, a delightful example of 18th-century Gothic. The picture shows the house when it was still lived in.

is perfectly symmetrical and the windows of classical proportions – the Gothic touches invlude Tudor hood moulds over the first floor windows while other windows have trefoil tracery in the upper panes. Everywhere the detail is engagingly playful with two sizes of battlements, curvilinear gables, and a very delicately detailed porch.

Behind the house are extensive pleasure grounds – the shrubs and trees suggest that they are largely Victorian but in the middle is an enchanting cylindrical summer house of two storeys with the upper storey approached by an outside flight of steps like that of a helter-skelter. Pevsner dates this to the 1630s but it seems more likely it is part of the love of the "true rust" associated with Sanderson Miller and his circle – this time looking back being not to the middle ages but the seventeenth century.

Ecton has been unoccupied since 1952, and the District Council had for some time been trying to persuade the Trustees, through

their agents, to carry out repair works. Under pressure from the District Council the Trustees had offered to sell the Hall and an adjoining area of garden to the Council. In July 1981, Kit Martin who had been interested in Ecton for some time produced a scheme for eleven houses and flats within the Hall and its outbuildings. The Trustees refused to sell on the grounds of "an inadequate price and an excessive land take". Yet when a listed building is compulsorily purchased following a Repairs Notice, the price reflects its condition, which in the case of Ecton is very poor.

The point at issue is whether the District Council will compulsorily purchase the outbuildings as well as the Hall as without them a conversion scheme will neither be practical nor viable.

On 16 August 1982 I wrote from SAVE to Wellingborough District Council once more pressing for action. The Council, I was told six weeks later, had "not lost sight of the problem". Late in 1981 they had commissioned " . . . an independent viability study in an attempt to establish what land and buildings should be included in a Repairs Notice as a prelude to compulsory acquisition, in order to produce a viable scheme for restoring the Hall". The result of this indicated that not only would the Hall and outbuildings be required but an additional area of land " . . . for providing five additional units". I could hardly believe it: once again the Council proposed to go down the tragic route of Finedon, now engulfed in a modern housing estate, by granting permission for new housing to make restoration "viable".

I then wrote to Michael Heseltine, Secretary of State for the Environment, urging him to use his reserve powers to serve a Repairs Notice on Ecton, as he had recently done at Barlaston Hall in Staffordshire. The reply came on 8 December 1982: "I naturally share SAVE's concern over the deterioration of any listed building due to lack of adequate repairs by the owner." But once again it was Catch 22. "As a Grade II listed building, I do not regard Ecton Hall as of sufficient importance to justify my exercising my powers." Mr. Heseltine asked the Borough Council to re-examine the use of its powers, but the stalemate has continued.

Ecton is a classic example of the inadequacy and ineffectiveness of Britain's planning laws. Here is an exceptionally attractive house, of considerable significance in the history of the Gothic Revival,

ABOVE: Ecton in 1983. The house, empty since the 1950s, is in an advanced state of dereliction behind the handsome garden front.

which has been allowed to deteriorate, even though a purchaser, with a proven record of rescuing large country houses, is eager and ready to buy the house – and has been for more than five years. As seen from the other cases discussed in this chapter show the lesson to be learnt is that you have to go on and on fighting and pressing for action. Re-examining the fate of these beautiful decaying houses, it is chilling to realise how often it has taken ten or fifteen years to find and implement a solution.

BUNTINGSDALE

On either side of the town of Market Drayton, which stands close by the Shropshire/Staffordshire border, are two more remarkably handsome houses whose plight is an object lesson in the disasters that can overtake houses of great quality and importance within a very short space of time. Both have highly unusual names – Buntingsdale and Pell Wall.

Buntingsdale has long been attributed to Francis Smith of Warwick (1672–1738), the most successful master builder in the history of British architecture whose name is associated with numerous fine houses all over the Midlands and beyond, built in the 1710's, 20's and 30's. In almost every case there are difficulties in defining Smith's precise role. In some instances he was simply the builder, working to a design by a leading architect such as James Gibbs. Elsewhere he himself appears to have been the architect, though at least sometimes his patrons also had a clear hand in the design. The lead rainwater heads at Buntingsdale carry the initials B.M. 1721 – standing for Bulkeley Mackworth whose family had acquired the estate in 1501. (Finedon it is sad to note was also a Mackworth estate.) Avray Tipping, writing in 1917 in *Country Life*, records there had been much " . . . valuable matter in the shape of actual notes and agreements between the owner and the architect . . . " when a north wing was added to the house in 1857. All these papers had been lent to the builder in charge of the alterations, a Mr. Smith of Shrewsbury – no relation of Francis Smith. This Mr. Smith never returned the papers but Tipping cites an agreement to provide Francis Smith with "a pad nag to ride hither from Warwick" to supervise the works.

Buntingsdale, Tipping wrote, stood in "rich pastoral country fairly level, but with steep-sided and often rocky water-worn hollows whose streams are easily formed into lakes". When I went to the house with Kit Martin early in March 1981 my first impression as we approached was very different – row upon row of RAF housing had been built over the estate to the south. A noble avenue, now with a neatly asphalted cycleway down the centre survived to suggest how grand Buntingsdale's setting had once been. I feared we were coming to a house where all sense of seclusion would have disappeared but as we drew close, the road veered off to the left past a lake beneath an overhanging cliff still "picturesquely bosomed in trees" as Tipping had described it in 1917. From here the road swung round to the entrance front, still as grand as it looked in the old *Country Life* photographs.

Francis Smith's country houses have two particular hallmarks – superb brickwork, almost invariably the strong red or pink characteristic of the early eighteenth century, and secondly very

ABOVE: Buntingsdale Hall, Shropshire in 1917. A fine example of the early 18th-century baroque. Its condition has deteriorated sharply in recent years.

distinctive baroque masonry details – principally doorcases – usually taken, or adapted from, plates in Rossi's *Architectura*, a superb collection of engravings of baroque buildings in Rome published between 1702 and 1721. Buntingsdale is an arch example of this. The doorcase, instead of the usual pediment over the door, had two fragments of pediment totally unconnected with each other. The front is ennobled with giant pilasters rising through two stories but plain pilasters are unexpectedly sandwiched between fluted ones. These were deliberate solecisms made by architects and patrons with a good knowledge of the grammar of classical architecture, who chose to break the rules to achieve unusual, even bizarre effects.

We had expected to find the house empty but work was evidently going on within. We inquired and discovered Buntingsdale was being converted into flats. This sounded good news but as we entered the room to the right of the hall we froze with horror. We had entered a large well-proportioned room with a bold cornice, and in the opposite corner a new staircase had been built rising straight through the ceiling, and filling the corner of the room in a brutish and clumsy fashion, while to make space for the upper flight, the cornice had been barbarously hacked away.

That day we penetrated no further but walking round the end of the house we stopped aghast once again. A doorway was being made in a window. Superb brickwork had been gouged out and the steps up to the new door were flanked with breeze block walls. Incensed at such treatment I immediately wrote to the local planning authority only to receive a firm assurance on 28 April 1981 that the work was quite satisfactory and would "ensure further useful life of the building". We had simply received a bad impression by arriving while work was going on; the walls to the steps were now being rendered – and only one of the main rooms had had a staircase put through the ceiling. The Council was glad to see a development probably ensuring "that the building will remain with every likelihood of proper maintenance".

A year later we received a very different letter from the Council. All work had come to a halt, the developer had disappeared and could we help with suggestions as to what could be done with the house. North Shropshire District Council, however, did not let matters rest there but used its powers to carry out emergency works.

How had Buntingsdale fallen on such hard times? Its builder Bulkeley Mackworth had died childless: his brother Sir Humphrey had a seat at Gnoll Castle in Glamorganshire. As Sir Humphrey had no interest in Buntingsdale it had passed to his cousin William Tayleur, with all the furniture, in the mid-eighteenth century. Tayleur's great grandson who succeeded in 1856 had remodelled and enlarged the house but according to Tipping " . . . the old work was kept where possible and the new work designed from it". Yet when I visited Buntingsdale again in 1983 and was able to look round the whole house there was no sign of the two very fine panelled rooms, illustrated in *Country Life* in 1917; a business room and a bedroom with characteristic early eighteenth-century corner chimneypieces. Indeed the whole house was so lacking in internal features, apart from the hall and staircase, that we wondered if there had not been a severe fire. However, this was not the case and it seems they were probably stripped out by the RAF which had acquired the estate in about 1936.

The house was to have been divided vertically into five separate units; and everywhere doors had been sealed off or opened up to make the units self-contained. The divisions had been made in the most curious way. The new houses did not run from one side of the building to the other, like terrace houses, but stood back to back – a blown-up version of the classic back to back houses in Leeds. More surprising the basement and offices had been blocked off so that the owners of the new houses had no access to rooms above and below them, and indeed no ready control over what happened there.

On the asset side, the setting of the house was better than I remembered. The entrance front looked out over fields. A decaying tennis court crudely sited just opposite the front door was a major eyesore. To the east were woods and to the south a very extensive lawn ending in a great semi-circle terrace overlooking the lake. The RAF housing was not intrusive. The problem of Buntingsdale now lay in divided ownership. One house had been sold off, a building society had foreclosed on another, the developer's interest had been seized by a creditor. Yet as I write there is hope that a trust may yet take over and restore the building as flats. But negotiating with several different owners creates hideous problems and meanwhile Buntingsdale continues to decay.

PELL WALL

The plight of Pell Wall is even more heart-rending than that of Buntingsdale, though once again it is not without hope. Sir John Soane, its architect, is recognized as the most original of all British architects, Vanbrugh only excepted. Yet Soane's work has suffered devastating casualties. His masterpiece, the great extensions to the Bank of England, was virtually destroyed during rebuilding between the wars. Pevsner's *London* calls this "the worst individual loss suffered by London architecture in the first half of the twentieth century". Soane's work at the House of Lords perished as a consequence of the burning of the Houses of Parliament in 1834. His remarkable law courts in Westminster were demolished in 1883. Of the eighteen wholly new country houses built to his designs, five have been completely demolished, five greatly altered and only eight survive in a relatively original condition. Pell Wall is important as the only country house produced in the last phase of Soane's life. "In composing the plans of this villa", Soane wrote, "my best energies have been exerted, intending that, when it was completed my private, professional labours should cease." Soane's drawings for Pell Wall survive in his house at 13 Lincoln's Inn Fields, today the Soane Museum. The records show the design was evolved patiently over some five years with a set of watercolour drawings of interiors surviving to show the intense care Soane devoted to every detail. His client was Percy Sillitoe, a solicitor, who Soane records in his *Public and Private Buildings* placed, "the most unbounded confidence" in him as architect.

With expectations thus aroused, the first sight of the estate, driving south from Market Drayton, comes as a devastating blow. There, beside the road, is Soane's gatelodge dwarfed by a large modern addition built on to it, completely out of tune in scale, materials and colour. In an instant the truth is apparent. The estate and grounds have been sold off as development lots. Yet the grounds prove to be unexpectedly thickly planted, renewing hope that the house may survive in some seclusion. A curving drive, now rampant with weeds, leads down to the entrance which at a first glimpse has the magic of a stage set. The forecourt is completely enclosed and the house suddenly stands abruptly in front of you. It is engagingly domestic in scale, rather like a fashionable *fin de siècle* private house in Paris standing in its own grounds on the Avenue Foch. This urbane look is not entirely fortuitous as the elegant entrance porch is, in fact, a turn of the century addition as the art nouveau grille in the lunette over the door makes clear. To the left is a blank wall, again with Soanian detail concealing what transpires to be a swimming pool. In the centre of the forecourt are the overgrown basins of a fountain. The colouring is intensely evocative – the steely grey of the stucco and the lush green of the shrubs. Julia Trevelyan Oman might have created it as a set for Covent Garden.

Plunging through the hedge, you emerge on the north front. Here Soane's elevation is intact, with a curving bow in the centre not to let in sun but to take advantage of the views across the valley to Market Drayton. The house here looks as if it is built of gigantic blocks of stone nearly two feet high and four or more feet long, like the blocks the Greeks used for the walls of their temples within the colonnades. At the upper level these are beautifully incised with a flat key pattern frieze. All this, it transpires, is simply a veneer of plaster over a brickwork shell. The lower windows of the bow curiously transpire to be blank – just where the principal saloon would normally be situated. Moving round, an explanation presents

BELOW: Pell Wall, Shropshire. The last country house designed by Sir John Soane. It has been empty and deteriorating since the 1950s.

itself – an addition, carefully matched to Soane's work, but with the remains of sumptuous mid-Victorian plasterwork. These additions and alterations, it emerges, were made after Percy Sillitoe's death in 1855: the house has passed through his niece to the Griffin family, and the work was probably done for Martin Harcourt Griffin who lived here from 1861 to 1880. For ten years from 1891 Pell Wall had been let. It had then been sold with 300 acres to James Munro Walker of the whisky family for whom the swimming pool and bachelor wing had been added.

According to Jackson-Stops and Staffs' sales particulars in 1964 it had been acquired in 1928 by the Brothers of Christian Instruction and used as a boys' boarding school until 1962. In 1965 the house was purchased by a Mr. Rolf, and from then the house had been largely left empty and deteriorating. Mr. Rolf had obtained planning permission to use the house as an entertainment and exhibition centre but this had not materialized. A decade later he applied for permission to demolish the house. The inspector, in his report following an inquiry in 1978, had concluded that "the possibilities of retaining and restoring" the house had not been fully explored, especially as the owner was unwilling to sell the whole property.

I went to the house for the second time in 1980 with Kit Martin, and this time we were able to explore the interior. What we found was not Soane's work but an extraordinarily lush, and richly detailed mid-Victorian interior arranged around a central atrium lit from above by a dome. In the bow on the north front, in place of Soane's drawing room an imperial staircase had been contrived – consisting of a short, straight flight branching into two and mounting in a gentle curve to a first floor landing. Between atrium and staircase was the neat conceit of a fireplace with a pane of glass above, the device Sir Charles Barry used in the hall of the Reform Club, the trick being that the smoke goes up a flue at the side of the fireplace.

We had arrived in a downpour and once inside found rain cascading through the central dome. Everywhere beautiful plasterwork was collapsing, or about to collapse. The timbers of the first floor landing were sodden and rotten: the situation looked desperate.

OPPOSITE: The Victorian ballroom at Pell Wall in 1978. Sumptuous plasterwork was beginning to crash down from the ceiling.

ABOVE: The north front of Pell Wall. Though parts of the grounds have been sold for development, the house is still secluded with a potentially attractive garden and a good view.

Yet the rooms around the landing were in much better condition and the roofs above were still in reasonable condition. In one upstairs room, Soane's original decoration survived complete with his "starfish" vaulted ceiling and chimneypiece. The attics, again on the outside of the central well, were quite dry though full of dirt and debris.

Two years later I again went to Pell Wall. This time the weather was much better and the house much drier. Surprisingly the plaster-work had deteriorated much less than I had expected. Following my visit with Kit Martin I had written suggesting the house could be converted into flats with the atrium acting as a shared entrance hall and flats opening off from the ground floor and gallery above. The Council received a further application to demolish from Mr. Rolf which went to the Planning Committee on 7 December 1982. The planning officer's resolve had strengthened, and a new attempt was set in motion to find someone willing to take on the house only a few months before demolition looked imminent.

There is now hope that a new national Buildings Preservation Trust, which has grown out of the highly successful Derbyshire Historic Buildings Trust, may take on the house. Once again the lesson is how long it takes to achieve action. The school moved out in 1962 and more than twenty years later Pell Wall is still rotting and empty.

BELFORD

The most poignant of all the empty and decaying country houses I have seen was one of the first I visited – Belford Hall in Northumberland. I visited the house in June 1968 while preparing some articles on the villas of James Paine for *Country Life*. Belford was owned by McLaren and Company, a firm of gravel extractors who had bought the estate in 1923 and operated a quarry a little way behind the house to the north. The shock came as I went inside to discover some of the most exquisite eighteenth-century plaster-work I had ever seen. Usually in a house like this the two or three main rooms might have elaborate decoration, but the rest of the house would be plainer. But here all the rooms on the main floor had superb ceilings – in very low relief, but immensely delicate. Each room was different, and the plasterwork continued on the first floor where the bedrooms all had very pretty cornices, each as I remember to a different pattern. Everywhere the detail was still beautifully crisp – almost as if it had never been repainted.

The house had been empty for some time and now the paint was flaking everywhere. In one of the main rooms the water had recently burst in through the cornice leaving only a ghastly mess of lath, looking like an appalling wound. For the rest, Belford was more or less intact though infinitely dingy. The floors in most places were sound, the doors still in good condition, even, I think, the chimneypieces. But the owners had no use for it, and there was no sign in this northern part of Northumberland of anyone at that time being willing to take on the house without the estate – which McLarens wished to maintain.

Belford had been built for Abraham Dixon in 1754–56.

Externally it is a handsome Palladian villa, with a central pediment supported on columns. But on closer examination the treatment is less conventional. In his early houses, the architect James Paine tended to crowd his fronts with architectural elements – pilasters, entablatures and pediments. Thus at Belford, one of his earlier designs, there are additional pilasters at either side of the portico, coupled pilasters at the angles, and the cornice of the first floor windows is carried along the main front as if it was strapping the house together. It is as if Paine was trying to develop a rationale to justify the use of classical orders on a flat elevation.

Paine's early patrons were centred on Newcastle and Doncaster and for the most part they were building with new money even if they came from old families. Abraham Dixon was just such an entrepreneurial spirit. *A View of Northumberland* published in 1811 records that when Belford came into his possession " . . . it consisted only of a few miserable cottages belonging chiefly to the adjoining farms, with a population of no more than a hundred". Dixon repaired the roads leading to Belford, set up a woollen factory and a tannery, and soon it was a flourishing small market town.

Paine had designed the house with attached wings but these were not built: a pair of wings were added by the architect John Dobson of Newcastle in 1818 for William Clark whose family were to retain the house until 1923, when it was sold to McLarens. The east wing, McLarens said, was in the process of being converted to flats when the house was requisitioned at the outbreak of the Second World War. A hutted camp was erected round the edge of the park, and the Hall served as the officers' mess. The army carried out some repairs and installed mains services. After the war the house continued to be used for various functions, including the local flower show and various dances.

When I went again to Belford in 1980 it was completely boarded up and I was not allowed inside. The superb ashlar stone was still in excellent condition, and behind the broken windows the eighteenth-century shutters were visible. However, elder trees were

OPPOSITE: The south front of Belford Hall, Northumberland, a handsome mid-18th-century Palladian house. Empty for many years, it has recently been sold to a restoration trust.

growing from the parapet and it was evident the roof was in appalling condition. At this time John Sambrook, an architect working for the Greater London Council's Historic Buildings Division, had taken an interest in the house, hoping to buy it and repair it gradually over the years. His report, dated March 1981, makes tragic reading. All the interior joinery except the window shutters had been removed, collapsed floors made it impossible to enter all the rooms – though dry rot at least was only evident in the basement vaults, and most of it was inactive. The really desperate part was that a rainwater pipe, housed in the internal wall, which took water from the valley roof, had been removed so that rainwater was discharging at the rate of 12,000 gallons-a-year onto the landing by the head of the stairs. John Sambrook's plans were dashed when the house was sold to another buyer. His interest and agitation may yet produce results, for the Civic Trust for the North East has formed a building preservation trust, the Northern Heritage Trust, which has drawn up plans to restore and convert Belford as flats. As I write they have just received a grant from the Monument Trust of £10,000 to buy the house, and for the first time in 15 years there is real cause for hope. The lesson again, is just how long it takes to secure action on even one beautiful derelict house.

STOCKEN HALL

Turning to the Midlands, just such a protracted struggle has taken place over Stocken Hall in Leicestershire which is all the more inexcusable as it belongs to a Government department. I had long known the house from photographs, but the opportunity to visit it came unexpectedly in 1979 when I was driving north with Sophie Andreae, Secretary of SAVE, along the stretch of the A1 north of Stamford which follows Ermine Street, on the way to the SAVE office at Hebden Bridge. We suddenly realized we were driving straight past Stocken. You turn off at Stretton, near the Ram Jam Inn, and the drive leads directly north out of the village. On the map it is clear the estate is large with no public roads across it, though the area around the house is no longer marked as parkland on the new Ordnance Survey. Stocken, we knew, belonged to the Home Office and was used as a prison farm for prisoners from the open prison at

Ashwell some miles away. Large notices at the gates threatened anyone proceeding with arrest. But it was the end of the afternoon and as we drove up a very long drive flanked by the remnants of a once-fine avenue there was no one in sight.

We arrived at the house and found a scene of spectacular squalor – rubbish and broken equipment strewn everywhere. We walked round to the garden side looking for the handsome 1740s front we knew from photographs. Passing a three-storey Victorian tower we peered through the windows and saw what appeared to have been until recently a canteen. Beyond was the handsome Georgian front attributed by John Harris to George Portwood, the most prominent of the master builders in Stamford. This is a beautifully jointed ashlar stone front with Gibbs windows – the name given to windows with emphatic blocked surrounds. We knew from the photographs of the interior that it had been vandalized beyond repair or recognition but the windows were shuttered and we could not see in. Although the Home Office had effectively abandoned the house to its fate, the actual structure remained in apparently sound condition.

I gleaned some historical details of the house from Roger Fleetwood-Hesketh who had been brought up there, and whose brother Peter had long been agitating about its condition. Stocken was said to have been built in the early seventeenth century by one Samuel Browne, of London origin. Parts of his house remain but early in the eighteenth century it was acquired by the Heathcotes who had recently bought the great estate at Normanton nearby. Sir Gilbert Heathcote (1652–1733), an early director of the Bank of England, was reckoned at his death to be the richest commoner in England. Towards the end of the eighteenth century the house had been the home of General Grosvenor who had married the daughter of the third Sir Gilbert.

However, extensive Victorian alterations including the gabled Victorian tower has been made by the then tenants, Lord Francis Cecil, the second son of the Marquess of Exeter. This work was probably done between his marriage in 1874 and his death in 1889. The Fleetwood-Heskeths acquired the estate in 1907 but left the house in 1940 when it was taken over by the RAF. Soon after the war the whole estate was acquired by the Home Office.

ABOVE: The early Georgian front of Stocken Hall, Leicestershire. The estate was acquired by the Home Office and used as a prison farm. The house was allowed to decay and but for the public outcry would have been demolished. Early in 1984 it was offered for sale and a number of firm offers were made.

By 1980 the Home Office were proposing to demolish Stocken Hall and a public inquiry was held in October of that year. Owing to the strength of public opposition, we heard on 2 July 1981 from the Assistant Secretary at the Department of the Environment that Michael Heseltine and William Whitelaw, then Home Secretary, had agreed that " . . . the Hall should be placed on the market for a period of six months." In other words, we and others were invited to produce a scheme for its future. As Kit Martin and I were then working on a book on this theme, *The Country House: to be or not to be* and had the bones of just such a scheme, we found ourselves a few weeks later in an office in Savile Row face to face with the representatives of the Home Office. What followed is worth relating as an amusing insight into the way the public sector works.

The meeting soon ran into difficulties with Kit Martin trying doggedly to establish why the Home Office had decided to site a new Young Offenders establishment a few hundred yards from the house. Quite apart from the prison farm next to the Hall, this major new prison, which was to have a high security perimeter fence all round, would greatly increase the blight on the house. As the estate was large we asked whether the new prison could not be sited elsewhere, where it would have less impact on the house. This, it was quickly made clear, was quite out of the question; contracts were about to be let and anyway there was no other suitable site. In any case, who were we to question the Home Office on the siting of new prison buildings. Further questioning elicited the fact that the new prison would at least be just over the brow of the hill, and with some additional planting might be screened from the house, though only a site visit could establish how effective this might be.

The second question concerned access. We believed that the house must have a separate drive if it was to be restored. Fortunately a track existed, leading directly north from the house through Forestry Commission land to a road connecting quickly with the A1. If you were driving from London it would mean traversing three sides of a square but from any other direction it was an excellent approach and it would save future occupants of the house from driving past all the depressing paraphernalia of the prison – as well as a new estate of prison officers' houses. The Home Office officials, it was clear, thought this a point of no consequence, vital though it was in our minds to the commercial viability of a scheme.

The next point at issue was the amount of land to be made available with the house. There were, we were told by the senior Home Office official, three options. The first option was that the house and small patch of lawn to the south would be offered for sale. The outbuildings behind the house would continue to be used for the prison farm and the purchasers of the house would have no access or right of way on that side. In other words they would have no control at all as to what happened immediately outside their windows. The second option was the same as the first except that the purchasers would have a right of way through the yard on the north side. Our reaction to these options was simple: they were hopeless. We moved to option three – the Home Office's most generous offer. This was to sell the house with about four acres of land and to move the pigsties from the outbuildings at the back to a site nearer other prison farm buildings, two or three hundred yards up the drive.

The Home Office would only do this if the Department of the Environment paid for new pigsties and a prisoners' urinal to boot. Under no circumstances was this to fall on the prison construction budget. And here was the catch. To move these pigsties would cost £900,000. All of us, including the Department of the Environment representatives, looked aghast: £900,000 for pigsties. Surely £300,000, ventured the man from the Property Services Agency. The senior Home Office official visibly stiffened. "I manage a building budget of £60 million a year. I know current building costs. I'm telling you these buildings will cost every penny of £900,000 by the time you've included 20 per cent architect's fees." Again we all started in amazement. Architect's fees at 20 per cent we exclaimed. "Architects, surveyors, quantity surveyors and other professional fees," we were told, "would certainly cost 20 per cent." But do you need architects to design pigsties, Kit Martin asked. Every farming magazine carries advertisements from suppliers who will measure up and install pigsties at minimal cost. And surely, Kit Martin pointed out, if you continue with your pigsty in that sixteenth- or seventeenth-century barn at the back of the house you're going to have to spend very substantial sums in repairs, year after year. "But that's maintenance," said the junior Home Office official. "The Treasury will always pay for maintenance, no matter how expensive." And he burst into a fit of giggles.

We were then asked if option three in terms of land was acceptable. The answer was no. The sale had to include more land. Then precisely how much was needed to make the house a viable proposition? We were unwilling there and then to draw a line on a map – first we had to look more closely at the position of the new prison, and second obviously we had to make a site visit. But suddenly all the officials from both departments were incensed. "You mean to say," we were told, "that when the Home Office has set out three options in detail you won't be specific. The Secretary of

OPPOSITE: The vandalized staircase at Stocken. All the original 18th-century bannisters have been broken and removed.

State will be very sorry that you are wasting his Department's time in this way, Mr Martin.'' But we stood our ground and duly sent in a map marking an area of fifteen to twenty acres of land we thought was the absolute minimum that should be made available with the house. Bob Weighton, Kit Martin's former partner, also went in to the question of the pigsties for us, measured them and costed replacements. Instead of £900,000 – or £300,000 – he produced a figure of £57,750 including fitting out, and builders' preliminaries – which a supplier might do at no cost, saving £5,250. These prices were for standard modern units, infinitely superior to the existing accommodation. If the pigsties were to be of the most sophisticated insulated construction, as advanced as any in Europe, the cost would be £73,000. These were duly sent to the Department of the Environment on 21 October 1981.

By a strange quirk of fate two years later to the day, 21 October 1983, the sale particulars for Stocken Hall arrived from Cluttons. The land offered was the Home Office's option three and no more. Purchasers would have to use the prison approach, not the new drive we suggested to the north. Offers of not less than £25,000 are invited for Stocken Hall, I read, with the coach house and outbuildings in about 4.2 acres. Yet the land without the buildings would be worth virtually nothing – as the Home Office would certainly object to anything being built there. And the house and outbuildings in their neglected, derelict state have a nil or minus value. So the price tag looks yet another obstacle to a proper solution.

There is obviously a possibility that someone will buy the house. A substantial country house at £25,000, or less, looks a bargain. But will the purchaser have the money to repair and adapt the house. Cluttons nonetheless had a very substantial number of inquiries in the first two months the house was on the market and one of the strongest contenders was a local scheme to use Stocken as a crafts centre. The saga of Stocken therefore is posed to continue.

THE GRANGE

The fate of few country houses has evoked such strong passions as The Grange in Hampshire. On 1 June 1972, just three months before the news broke that it was to be blown up with dynamite, J. Mordaunt Crook had written in *Country Life*:

"The architectural roll-call of the Grange is second to none: William Samwell, Robert Adam, Henry Holland, William Wilkins, George Dance, Sir Robert Smirke, no less than three members of the Cockerell dynasty – S.P., C.R. and F.P. – as well as a shadowy Victorian named John Coxe, all these were involved in the history of the house between the late 17th and late 19th century."

On September 8, *The Sunday Times* had quoted Sir John Summerson, curator of the Soane Museum who is far from always to be found on the side of preservation, as saying: "Everybody realizes this is an extremely important building in the history of English and European architecture. It cuts us to the quick to throw away this building."

The saga of the saving and repair of The Grange is an immensely complex story with many protagonists but when on 29 July 1983 *The Times* published a short report announcing it was now restored and open to the public, it said simply the house had "continued to decay until 1979 when, after appeals from the President of the Royal Academy, the Society of Antiquaries and the Council for British Archaeology, the Secretary of State set aside £500,000 to restore the house". This seemed a rather abbreviated version of what at SAVE had been a remarkable and tense drama as well as an amazing revelation of the way Ministers, or their senior civil servants, can try to duck out of responsibilities they have solemnly taken on.

I turned to the SAVE file and the first item I came to was a solicitor's document, with the characteristic vertical fold, headed:

IN THE HIGH COURT OF JUSTICE QUEEN'S BENCH DIVISION TO THE DIVISIONAL COURT IN THE MATTER OF An application for leave to apply for judicial review by Peter Burman Marcus Binney and Timothy Cantell for themselves and as trustees of The SAVE Britain's Heritage Trust and by John Redmill and IN THE MATTER OF The Grange Northington in the County of Hampshire.

With this was an affidavit beginning "I Marcus Binney, architectural journalist . . . make oath . . . ", setting out the facts pertinent to our action.

On 13 March 1974 the Department of the Environment had issued a press notice announcing that the owner of The Grange, the

Hon. John Baring, had offered the house "in voluntary guardianship, along with a contribution to the cost of repairs." Two days later the Department had written to John Redmill confirming the position: "although general admission to the public will not be possible for some considerable time because of the need for extensive repairs it is hoped to arrange for people with specialist interest in the building to visit as soon as the legal formalities have been completed". As further evidence we attached a copy of the guardianship deed by which the Secretary of State came under a duty to maintain the building and a right of access was conferred on the public. Between 1975 and 1978, the affidavit continued, John Redmill had made regular inquiries as to when work would begin and was generally told it was hoped to do so in the near future.

We then quoted from an unusually candid letter from the Department dated 12 October 1978. "I think that what your letter boils down to, is the question why has the Directorate of Ancient Monuments and Historic Buildings apparently done nothing to conserve The Grange since it was taken into the Secretary of State's guardianship in 1975, since when it has disintegrated considerably." The letter continued: "While it is not for me to anticipate the Minister's timetable, I expect that Lady Birk may be taking a final decision . . . within the next month or two."

The writ and the affidavit I quote from were never served. In the end the threat proved enough but only after SAVE's solicitor at the time, Mr. Robert Trotter of Bates, Wells and Braithwaite had been daily ready to go to the High Court for several weeks.

Quite why The Grange had been so scandalously left to rot is still not clear – there was a change of Government in February 1974 and this perhaps allowed senior civil servants to backpedal on a decision of the outgoing Minister of which they had never approved. Their tactic appeared simple: to let the building decay till costs became prohibitive and the Minister then decided it was no longer a proper use of public funds.

Advised by Robert Carnwath, our solicitors had written on 8 December 1978 to the Secretary of State calling for a categorical assurance that the Department would immediately take all necessary steps to preserve the building from further decay during the winter, also specifying what works would be carried out in the future. As might be expected the Department gave no such assurance but sought a meeting.

Ten days later we found ourselves with our solicitor in the office of Mr. Maurice Mendoza, the Under-Secretary in charge of Ancient Monuments who explained that The Grange "had not been the easiest case for the Department. It was not a monument we would have expected to take on". They had a scheme to preserve it but the Government had put a moratorium on all contracts. The Department was, however, recosting the scheme and there were two possibilities: to preserve as much of the building as was practical, putting a light roof on to protect it. Secondly, they would simply preserve the portico, and reduce the remaining walls to a "safe" level. This second opinion, we made clear, was wholly unacceptable. The two schemes we were told would both be put to the Minister, who would hopefully make a decision early in the New Year. It would be mid-January before anyone could be on site.

Two days later our solicitors wrote to the Department agreeing to postpone action till 1 February, but making it clear that "if a satisfactory decision had not been taken by the end of January we shall apply . . . for a writ of *Mandamus*". *Mandamus* is a basic right of all citizens to apply for a judicial order obliging a minister to carry out his statutory duties. "Our clients," the letter continued, "are most unhappy that any further period should pass by when The Grange is unprotected and open to further rapid deterioration. No satisfactory reason has been given for the inactivity of your Department over the years in which The Grange has been within guardianship."

By 1 February nothing had happened, only a request for more time. Reluctantly we gave it, on an almost daily basis until on 22 February 1979 we received the long-awaited assurance that Peter Shore, the Secretary of State had at last authorized the Department to proceed with repairs.

As usual, the Department moved forward unbelievably slowly. By the time of the election in June 1979 the Department had done no

OVERLEAF: The Grange in Hampshire, 1978. Saved from demolition in 1972, shortly before it was due to be dynamited, this great neo-classical house was taken into guardianship by the Department of the Environment, with a view to restoring it as a monument and opening it to the public. Four years later it was still abandoned and decaying.

more than scaffold the building to the level of the first floor windows. Then on 16 October came a bombshell – a press notice stating that Michael Heseltine, the Secretary of State in the new Conservative government was reviewing the whole matter and considering a range of options including leaving the building "to decay un-repaired" and demolishing it. Once again our solicitors wrote but Michael Heseltine's press release was also a public challenge to justify the preservation of the building in architectural terms. This we immediately set out to do in a lightning SAVE report *Ten Days to Save The Grange* – tied to the closing date of 31 November which Michael Heseltine had allowed for representations.

In September 1972 the news that The Grange was to be dynamited had provoked a furious correspondence in *The Times*. Fortuitously the news had broken on the eve of the opening of the great Council of Europe exhibition of Neo-classicism at The Royal Academy. On 9 September 1972 the Secretary General of the Council sent a dramatic midnight telegram to the Prime Minister, Mr Edward Heath, expressing the Council of Europe's "deep concern at the imminent destruction of one of Europe's great neo-classical monuments."

When I first arrived at The Grange late in September 1972, the slates had just been stripped from the roof but inside the house appeared in sound condition – wallpaper was peeling from the walls but the floorboards were sound and it was possible to walk round both upstairs and downstairs rooms without much difficulty. But many of the main architectural fittings had already been stripped out, including C.R. Cockerell's remarkable dining room, which David Watkin has described as "one of the most elegant and scholarly rooms of the whole Greek Revival. Based ultimately on the cella of the Temple at Bassae, it achieved that jewelled, casket-like quality which we know Cockerell felt was characteristic of Greek design." No less remarkable was the survival of elements of an earlier Charles II house by William Samwell, including an early and ingenious example of an Imperial staircase – one flight branching into two. These Samwell interiors had been described by Horace Walpole in the mid-eighteenth century as "beautiful models of the purest and most classic antiquity."

When William Wilkins had remodelled the house in 1805–09 for the young Henry Drummond he had simply encased the seventeenth-century house in Regency stucco. Yet out of the challenge had come not an uneasy compromise but a commanding masterpiece of immense assurance. Wilkins seized on the drama of the site – on a promontory looking down to a lake – and added a majestic Greek portico to the east flank of the Samwell house. With most Georgian houses the portico is in the middle of the long front. Here it fills instead the shorter side, so that seen from below the house does indeed look like a recreation of a Greek temple in an idyllic pastoral setting. Wilkins also showed his first hand knowledge of Greek architecture by setting the building on a sharply defined plinth with formal flights of steps leading down steeply between massive stone pedestals – giving it that sense of elemental geometric volumes that make the climb up to the Acropolis so memorable.

"In terms of international neo-classicism," I had written in the SAVE leaflet, "The Grange compares in architectural and historical importance to the Madeleine in Paris or the Admiralty building in Leningrad. It is to the history of country house design what David's Oath of the Horatii is to the history of painting or Canova's Maria Christina Monument in Vienna is to funerary sculpture". The house had exerted a magical effect on C.R. Cockerell when he first visited it in 1823. "Viewed it from the ground opposite . . . nothing can be finer more classical or like the finest Poussino, it realises the most fanciful representations of the painters pencil or the poet's description."

Michael Heseltine's gauntlet, inviting people to say whether they thought the restoration of The Grange was still worthwhile, produced a very strong response – virtually all vigorously in favour of preservation.

In December 1979 he announced The Grange would be preserved. Both the house and the conservatory would be roofed and made structurally sound. This was glorious news, but even then work proceeded unbelievably slowly, as if someone hoped against hope that the restoration could still be prevented. Almost a year later I was told by the Department of the Environment: "As far as physical work is concerned, we have completed most of the

preliminaries, including a small amount of excavation to reveal the earlier building, the clearance of vegetation, fencing and scaffolding." Yet the scaffolding had been half way up the building exactly a year before. But on 24 November 1980 came the long-awaited news: a contract had been let.

The opening of The Grange took place with remarkably little fanfare. A Department of the Environment Press Release on 24 May 1983, announced the house would at last be open to the public, on 26 May, just two days later. The photographs issued indeed showed a remarkable transformation. Four months later in the gathering dusk, I had the opportunity to see the house for myself. When I had visited the house in 1978, it had been in a desperate state – whole sections of the stucco on the columns of the portico had crashed to the ground; the coffering of the ceiling inside the portico had virtually disintegrated. But now The Grange was again in pristine condition. The bewitching stillness that all great houses have at dusk was here increased, knowing that inside it was completely empty. By making the house an ancient monument, it had become what its builders had intended, an essay in pure form – a Greek temple, silent and majestic, transposed into an English landscape.

DINGLEY HALL

In recent years the decaying shells of a number of abandoned houses have been restored and reoccupied. None more dramatically than Dingley Hall in Northamptonshire: a beautiful but ruined house which has been brought back to life without a penny of public money.

I arrived at Dingley unexpected early one Sunday evening in September 1979, and met Kit Martin for the first time, little knowing then it was to lead not only to an article in *Country Life*, but to a joint book on the rescue of problem houses three years later. He had acquired Dingley in 1976, and reconstruction was now well under way.

OPPOSITE: A room in The Grange in 1972. Work on stripping the house had begun but despite vandalism, the plasterwork survived largely intact. OVERLEAF: The Grange in 1983 soon after repairs were completed.

In 1958 the sales particulars had announced that the house " . . . is in an exceptional state of repair and has been consistently well maintained." Yet fifteen years later, after passing through a series of ownerships, Dingley was a wreck. Panelling, doors, doorcases, chimneypieces had been stripped out, the stone flags on the floors of the main ground floor rooms had gone, slates had been lifted from the roof, followed by the removal of almost all internal walls, floorboards and ceilings. Whole chimney stacks were collapsing as a result the loss of lateral support, bringing down large sections of the roof as they fell.

All this time Dingley was listed as Grade I – the top grade accorded to about only 5000 buildings in England – yet neither the local authority or the Department of the Environment had been able, or indeed willing, to stop the systematic wrecking of the house. Dingley owed its survival through this bleak period, I learnt, to a local farmer, Bob Skelton, who with a number of villagers, had kept up the gardens during these years.

Kit Martin had set up practice in Cambridge in 1969, before he had finished his training, with Bob Weighton, and together they had established a reputation rescuing and converting old buildings. He had first seen Dingley in 1975 and initial advice suggested it was a wholly impractical proposition. But he pressed ahead and acquired the house, calculating that he could hardly be refused planning permission. His plan was to reconstruct the house internally to form 14 self-contained houses (later the number was reduced to 10), leaving the exterior elevations unaltered. Negotiations over planning permission and building regulations took more than a year, and though there were indications that the work would qualify for a substantial repair grant from the Historic Buildings Council, the discussions proved so protracted he decided to proceed on his own before any more of the building collapsed.

His principle had been to tackle the building in stages, five in all, enabling him to recycle capital as the first parts were completed and sold. This also meant that the various trades could follow each other through the house and he could build up most of his own direct labour team which would be continuously employed on most aspects of the work. And while contractors' estimates for any aspect of work on the whole building would have been colossal, those for smaller stages, no larger than the average house, were more reasonable.

Kit had begun work on the early Elizabethan wing which he had converted into a house for himself, and the tower block at the back. These were the parts in worst condition on which there was least hope of a viable return. But once the first three houses had been completed strong interest developed in all the remaining units, and almost all of them were sold before they were completed – some even before they were begun.

His principle was to create a series of self-contained houses each with its own front door. The plan of Dingley – roughly an H – suited this approach. It was possible to make most of the new entrances in the rear court where rough walls had been left exposed by the demolition of a Victorian wing – demolished before he acquired the house. This meant that the formal gardens to the south and the lawns on the entrance side could be left undisturbed, so that the main elevations and their setting remained unchanged.

BELOW: Dingley Hall in Northamptonshire in 1979. The house was approaching collapse in 1976 when this photograph was taken.

His own house in the Elizabethan wing was modern inside and he had ingeniously added an extra bedroom on the roof, largely concealed behind the half-moon battlements. Living room, dining room and kitchen were on the first floor with spare rooms below.

This wing was dated 1560 – two years after Elizabeth I came to the throne but was carved with the unexpected inscription 'God Save the King'. As Edward VI had died in 1553 this is hard to explain except as a reference to Queen Mary's husband Philip II of Spain, hardly a popular figure in England even then. The wing had been built for Sir Edward Griffin who had been appointed Solicitor General by Henry VIII in 1546, promoted to Attorney General by Edward VI in which position he continued under Queen Mary. His strong papist leanings evidently lost him the appointment on Elizabeth's accession and he seems to have belonged to the group of recusants in northern Northamptonshire which included the Treshams of Rushton nearby. Edward Griffin and his brother were both included in a list of great letters [hinderers] of religion submitted by Bishop Scambler in 1564.

The evidence suggests that Sir Edward's house was built round a courtyard, with relatively few windows on the outside – what Mark Girouard has described as the inward-looking houses of the early years of Elizabeth's reign. Only a wing and a two-storey porch (dated 1558) survive from the Elizabethan house; for Dingley was radically remodelled in the 1680s by another Sir Edward Griffin who was Treasurer of the Chamber to Charles II and James II, and a fervent Jacobite. The handsome south and west ranges he added are usually ascribed to the gentleman architect, Hugh May. Edward Griffin's sister Anne had, in fact, married Hugh May's cousin. May is best known for his work at Eltham Lodge in Kent and Cornbury in Oxfordshire and the state rooms (now lost) he created at Windsor Castle. But as I studied the house I was increasingly struck by the similarity of the south front, particularly the unusual spacing of the windows, to a design for Combe Abbey in Warwickshire supplied to Lord Craven by another gentleman architect, Captain William Winde, and to the south front of Belton House which is also attributed

OPPOSITE: The roof terrace above the early Elizabethan wing at Dingley. A new rooftop bedroom is concealed behind the elaborate gables of the parapet.

to Winde. On this basis I tentatively reattributed the remodelling of Dingley to Winde – always a rash thing to do but I had a letter from Howard Colvin, author of the great *Biographical Dictionary of British Architects 1600–1840* which no architectural historian in Britain can live without. He said he had found a piece of evidence in the Combe Abbey correspondence which went some way to confirm the attribution. The joiner Captain Winde employed both at Combe and Castle Bromwich was John Sims, a Londoner. Among the letters was one from Sims dated September 22, 1686 about some money owing to him for work at Combe. It was written from Dingley with the implication that Sims was also working for Winde there.

Later in the seventeenth century Dingley had passed to the Hungerford family who had made the extensive additions at the back which have been demolished. In 1883 the house had been acquired by Viscount Downe who sold it to Earl Beatty, hero of the Battle of Jutland. Lord Beatty's main work was to lay out the terraced gardens to the south.

Two years after I first visited Dingley, Kit Martin completed work on the house, and moved to Gunton House in Norfolk, another much larger house in a perilous state which he is now restoring and converting. But my first chance visit to Dingley had indirectly another happy result. I had been on my way to the Hazells in Bedfordshire, then threatened with demolition. Following the public inquiry the Secretary of State, Michael Heseltine, refused permission to demolish the house and soon after Kit Martin acquired it. As I write the work of repair and conversion is well on the way to completion. Now he is searching in earnest for another major house to restore.

BARLASTON HALL

There can not be many people who are offered substantial eighteenth-century country houses for a pound, but this was the choice I was faced with, woken from a deep slumber at six o'clock in the morning of 29 September 1981, while staying in Atlanta, Georgia. Sophie Andreae was on the line, and of course it was eleven o'clock in England. "Wedgwood have just offered Barlaston

Hall to SAVE for a pound. Do we accept?"

She was in the middle of a public inquiry considering Wedgwood's application for consent to demolish Barlaston, a Grade I listed building. We had concentrated great efforts in the preparation of the case for the defence. Kit Martin's former partner Bob Weighton had drawn up a scheme showing how the house could be restored and converted into seven flats– on a viable commercial basis, and Peter Dann and Partners, structural engineers in Cambridge, had produced a scheme to show how the building could be protected from the effects of coal mining subsidence in the future.

Guided by David Cooper of Gouldens, our Solicitor, they had put forward such a strong case that Wedgwood's QC on the second day of the second week of the inquiry had flung down the gauntlet at what he scornfully referred to as "the United Aesthetes" challenging us to buy Barlaston for one pound sterling. The terms were simple. We had to complete the restoration and conversion within six years or Wedgwood would have the option to buy the building back for a pound. The offer was freehold with about one and three-quarters acres of land.

One pound may sound a bargain, but the problems of Barlaston were serious. First there was sheer decay. No repairs or maintenance had been carried out for a long time and during the last few years water had begun to pour through the roof. But the real problem was the subsidence. Barlaston stands above what the National Coal Board proudly claims to be one of the richest coalfields in Europe. Mining had begun in 1968/7 and seven more seams, some very deep, were to be mined over the next twenty years.

The whole village of Barlaston was likely to sink up to 40 feet in the process. The problems of Barlaston Hall were increased because it sat astride a "fault" – a geological change and there was the likelihood of differential settlement, of different parts of the house sinking to different levels or at different angles, causing cracks and compression. It sounds a nightmare, but it was possible to devise a structural system to protect the house.

Michael Heseltine had served notice on the Coal Board in July 1981 that he deemed Barlaston Hall "outstanding" – which potentially laid certain obligations on the Board – and at the inquiry the

Coal Board had produced a scheme showing how the house could be underpinned – at huge expense. Peter Dann and Partners had produced an alternative cheaper scheme which met heavy flak from the Coal Board but Peter Dann was nonetheless able to amend it to meet criticisms.

I then talked to David Cooper, our solicitor: he took the view we ought to accept Wedgwood's offer. If we didn't, where was our credibility. My first reaction was suspicion. If we ended up by having to buy a building every time we went to a public inquiry we would soon have a whole village on our hands. But I could see the force of what they said and for me there was one additional and compelling reason for accepting.

Barlaston Hall was almost without question the work of the architect Sir Robert Taylor (1714–88). There was no documentary evidence to prove this but the parallels with his other buildings were so numerous, and so close, that it was as sure as an attribution ever can be. I had written my BA thesis for the tripos at Cambridge on Sir Robert in 1966, and this had led me to my job at *Country Life* so not only did I owe Sir Robert much, but the attraction of being involved directly in work on one of his buildings was enormous.

In Atlanta it was still dark outside and I wanted time to reflect, but Sophie needed an answer. She was in a coin box and the chances of getting through two or three hours later when the transatlantic lines got busy were slim – and there was no way I could call her. So I agreed.

Three days after I returned from America, on 9 October, I made my first visit to Barlaston as a director of Starside – the company in which Sophie Andreae and David Cooper had vested the house pending the formation of a Barlaston Hall Trust. To own a building, however derelict, is to be in control of its future – at last there was no problem of asking for permission to visit the house: we could go whenever we wanted. My excitement and anticipation were immense.

Barlaston, although an austere building, does not disappoint. The approach is at right angles along an avenue of majestic limes and the house appears suddenly on the left standing some forty yards from the road. A fine Palladian house which has no gates, no wall, no fence, but simply a stretch of lawn running back from the road, is

rare in England. On the east coast of America it is common to see a
large classical town house set amidst open lawns without fences
of any kind. It happens at Barlaston because the road past the
hall is really a private drive. Today it has become one of the
approaches to the Wedgwood factory, although the avenue, shrubs
and neatly-mown verges make it clear it is no ordinary road.

There is an element in English taste always to prefer simplicity
over elaboration, elegance before richness, and to react against an
abundance of ornament. Barlaston is deliberately understated in just
this way. It is of Palladian proportions with a central pediment and
the one-three-one rhythm of windows which is characteristic of
Palladio's villas (what in the United States is called a five-part
house). Built of red brick rather than stone or stucco, the house is
without the giant portico that is the principal hallmark of Palladian
villas all over Europe and North America.

The nobility of the entrance front rests principally in its proportions. Palladian villas in Italy usually have only one storey above
the main floor, or *piano nobile*, often with smaller attic windows as
there are on the top floor of Barlaston. Here Taylor had to introduce
an extra floor for the principal bedrooms, and the brilliance of his
proportions is that the house seems neither top heavy nor too
high-waisted which happens when proportions go wrong. The
simplicity of Barlaston is alleviated in an unexpected way – the
unusual octagon and diamond pattern of the sash windows. This is a
hallmark of Sir Robert Taylor's work in the 1750s – an architectural
counterpart to Chinese Chippendale in furniture – both responses to
the craze for the Rococo which swept England from the continent in
the mid-eighteenth century. While Taylor's other buildings of the
1750s had largely lost their octagonal sashes, or been destroyed
altogether, at Barlaston the sashes remained – the glass broken, but
the woodwork surprisingly complete. On the ground floor they
had been boarded up by Wedgwood against vandals, but on the
upper floors they were still visible, and almost all of them we found
survived and could be repaired.

When you look closely at Barlaston you find it bears the most
extraordinary scars – a testimony in a way to all it has suffered. The
story goes that in the late eighteenth century a Duchess of Sutherland
was on her way to the ducal seat at Trentham, little more than a mile

ABOVE: The south front of Barlaston Hall in Staffordshire early in 1982. This handsome mid-18th-century Palladian villa had been neglected for many years until it was acquired in 1981 by SAVE Britain's Heritage for one pound sterling. OPPOSITE: Looking up to the roof of Barlaston in 1982. Floorboards had been removed, ceilings had collapsed and the main timbers were eaten away by rot.

up the road. "*What* is that vulgar red brick house on the hill over there?" she is reputed to have said in disparaging tones. Barlaston's owners, hearing the story, had the house rendered in fashionable stucco. And thus Barlaston had remained for a century and a half

until, Sophie Andreae found out, the Bank of England took over the house in the Second World War. Feeling the brilliant stucco made the house an eye-catcher to enemy aircraft, the Bank had it all removed. When you look at the brickwork today every brick has been neatly scored three or four times to provide a ground for the plaster – the hatching varies from one part of the building to another and clearly several craftsmen were involved. What must they have thought of their task – chiselling away at exceptionally fine brick-work only a few decades old.

On that October day it was the inside of Barlaston that I really wanted to see. Our concern was to find out how bad a state it was in and, more important, how much of the eighteenth century plaster-work and woodwork remained. The hall floor was cluttered with debris – part accumulated rubbish, part plaster and lath fallen from the ceilings. But here and there the original characteristic eighteenth-century stone paving was visible. The octagon pattern of the windows recurred as a *Leitmotif* throughout the house in the doors, shutters, and even the library bookcases.

In all the rooms on the main floor substantial amounts of plasterwork remained. The ornamental work had been concentrated on the walls rather than the ceilings which had been completely plain – so the collapse of large parts of ceiling was not as serious as it might have been. In all the main rooms sections of Taylor's elaborate cornices survived, as well as elaborately-moulded chairrails and skirtings. In the dining-room graceful rococo cartouches, which had formed the surrounds to large canvases inset in the end walls, were virtually intact. The lower flight of the main staircase had collapsed under the weight of falling plasterwork but we were able to explore the house further using the secondary stairs – ascending to the intriguing arcaded and cross vaulted landing which ran round the main staircase on three sides.

Below the main floor all was pitch dark as the windows were boarded up, but scrambling through piles of debris we discovered there were two levels of basement rooms. The first level was really a ground floor, as on three sides it opened directly onto the garden

OPPOSITE: Overmantel in the dining room at Barlaston in 1981. The chimneypiece had been torn out but the rich plasterwork above survived remarkably intact.

ABOVE: Another view of the dining room at Barlaston in 1981 showing the condition of the house before restoration began.

which was lower than the lawn in front of the house, while below this were further vaulted rooms.

That day Sophie had arranged for Swan and Partners of Kingsland, Herefordshire, builders whose work she knew, to come and put new locks on the house and make it secure. This was a fortunate choice as the two partners of the firm, Marc Cameron-Swan and Barry Morgan were immediately enthused by Barlaston and attracted to the idea of working on a major eighteenth-century house. A week later they began work on site and have been there ever since. As Barlaston was in appalling condition it was crucial that the work was supervised and directed on the spot by someone with a real understanding of eighteenth-century building, and since that October Barry and Marc have alternated, week by week, so that one of them has always been at Barlaston.

The first task was to get a proper roof on the house – water was pouring in and the interior was sodden. It had to be a temporary roof but the Historic Buildings Council came forward with the offer of a grant of £27,000 towards emergency work. The winter of 1981–82 was especially bitter – with snow on the ground for months, yet for all that time Swan and Partners worked patiently on the roof in appalling conditions until the whole house had a temporary protective roof. Just how damp the house had been only became clear with time – it was not until the summer of 1983 that to me it at last felt really dry.

In 1982 The Historic Buildings Council recommended the offer of a grant of a further £150,000 towards the full repair of the house. This was wonderful news but we soon learnt there was a catch. No payments would be made until the National Coal Board had agreed its contribution towards "preventitive measures" – designed to protect the building from further subsidence damage. Early in 1982 our engineers had received a six-page "schedule of conditions at Barlaston Hall". Dated 26 January this document listed 72 items which it said "are believed to be the only defects which can possibly be attributed to mining damage". A further letter from the Estates Manager of the Western Area of the National Coal Board on 23 February stated: "the Board's Architect's and Quantity Surveyor's assessment of the cost of the work detailed was in excess of £100,000."

At about this time we changed our engineers and architects to two London firms – to Brian Morton of Brian Morton and Partners as engineers, and Edward Burd of Hunt Thompson Associates as architects. Bob Weighton and Paul Riddington who had served us so well at the Inquiry both worked from Cambridge. Bob Weighton was now moving to Oundle and our lines of communication would become even more stretched at a time when we needed to have constant meetings, often at short notice, with our professional advisers.

After further discussions with the Historic Buildings Council we received permission to go ahead with permanent repairs, even though the money would not be released until agreement was reached with the Coal Board. In March Brian Morton sent his initial proposals for the preventitive measures to the National Coal Board who, shortly after told us that they would submit these for approval to independent consultant engineers. To our surprise, approval in principle came remarkably quickly – in April. Mining was due to begin again in August and we now urged the National Coal Board to allow us to put in emergency steel ties to protect the building from further subsidence damage. We were able to do this during the summer, with the National Coal Board paying some £47,000 for the work. After this work had been completed negotiations became still more protracted as the National Coal Board now demanded "we put all the money on the table", whereas formerly they had simply requested that we demonstrated the scheme was viable. At the Coal Board's request a meeting of all parties was held at the Department of the Environment in March 1983, chaired by Mrs. Jennifer Jenkins, the Chairman of the Historic Buildings Council. We were able to show we had financial resources to cover all the work except that associated with mining subsidence but still the Coal Board would not move. On 11 April, I wrote to Tom King, Michael Heseltine's successor, asking him to intervene. The announcement then came of the General Election and I received a brief but friendly note saying he was asking one of his senior officials to take over the matter. Another meeting was arranged with the Coal Board – on 20 July, this time, attended by the Coal Board's Deputy Secretary.

Once again we were at loggerheads. However, the official Minutes of the meeting note the key phrase to us: "Provided that SAVE sent the extra information promised during the meeting, he [the Deputy Secretary] would try to ensure that the Coal Board gave a speedy decision." This information was sent off shortly after, and over the next four months I telephoned at regular intervals the Deputy Secretary's Office and was always told a decision would be made shortly or as soon as possible. The decision, we understood, would be taken by a sub–committee of the full Board.

Then on Tuesday 8 November I had the opportunity to go and see the new Secretary of State for the Environment, Mr. Patrick Jenkin, for a general talk. I asked him first about Barlaston and his response was hearteningly positive. "I'll write to Mr. Macgregor at once," he said. And the letter he sent on 16 November was firm and clear, concluding that:

"Further delay is now putting the fabric of the building and the chances of financing its repair at risk, as well as threatening to render nugatory the very considerable costs and effort which have been incurred in keeping the building standing. I would therefore be very grateful if you could find time to look into the matter personally and see if a favourable decision could not now be reached."

We did not see Mr. Macgregor's reply, but understood it was sharp and suggested that he saw no good reason why he should be put under pressure in this way. The correspondence continued and on 9 March I heard from Patrick Jenkin that Mr. Macgregor's latest reply "has not taken us much further". And now a miners' strike was looming.

The good news was that work on the house was proceeding extremely well. In January 1984 Sophie Andreae's progress report was published in the *Staffordshire Historic Buildings Trust Newsletter*. The full repair of the roof was complete. New hand-made bricks from the Bulmer Brick and Tile Company had arrived in the summer of 1983 and cracked window arches were now being made good. Taylor's characteristic octagonal sashes were being repaired – surprisingly these were found to be of oak. By the early Spring all the signs were that we would be able to take down the scaffolding in the summer, and reveal the exterior to the world, restored to its former splendour.

On 1 April the new Commission on Historic Buildings and Monuments took over the work of the Historic Buildings Council. That very day *The Sunday Times* colour supplement carried a prominent article leading with a photograph of the Commission's new Chairman, Lord Montagu of Beaulieu. On the next page was a superb picture of Barlaston, taken for *The Sunday Times* shortly before we acquired the house. Barlaston Hall, the caption ran, " . . . has benefited from generous grants from the Historic Buildings Council". How ardently I wished this was true!

As I write, there is a real possibility that all work will have to be halted but even if it does the roof and the walls will be sound. The threat of demolition has passed but the battle of Barlaston, which began in earnest sixteen years ago following Andor Gomme's article on the house in *Country Life* in 1968, looks poised to continue.

CALKE ABBEY

The story of Calke Abbey in Derbyshire illustrates how the fate of a great, but remote, house, hitherto unknown can become a national issue within weeks. I first saw Calke Abbey on a November day in 1978. It was one of the most unknown and inaccessible country houses in England, and one of the very few major houses which had never been featured in *Country Life*. I had been staying in Derbyshire, on my way to look at mills in the Pennines and noticed Calke marked nearby on the ordnance survey. To my surprise, there was a little line of red dots indicating a public footpath leading towards the house from the west. I walked slowly up over fields until I reached the edge of the park and there below, surrounded on all sides by a vast park, was the house: beyond was a great lake, and to the right a little estate church perched on a hill. There was no-one in sight and we were just about to descend into the park when I noticed, walking slowly but purposefully towards me a tweedy figure with a shotgun under his arm. We had arrived on the day of a shoot, and clearly could go no further. The chance to return came in June 1982, when the future of Calke was well on the way to becoming a national issue. This time I was with John Harris and Gervase Jackson Stops.

A long drive from London always heightens anticipation. We were put in the mood by stopping two or three miles before the gates, on the hill that looks down to Staunton Harold in the north of Leicestershire. "For position," Pevsner says, "Staunton Harold, the house and chapel are unsurpassed in the country, certainly as far as Englishness is concerned." The sight of the handsome pedimented front with a beautiful gothic church on the lawn, reflected in a lake immediately below is all that Pevsner claims.

The first view of Calke stands up well even against Staunton Harold. Parkland sweeps down to the great baroque front. No Repton or Barry ever came to introduce a more formal setting of

ABOVE: Calke Abbey in the summer of 1983. House, contents, park and enough land to endow it for the National Trust had been offered in settlement of Capital Transfer Tax.

terraces, parterres and balustrades to set off the architecture. The entrance front, with its even rows of windows, gives away nothing of what lies within. Curiously, there are no steps up to the portico. The main entrance is beneath. The portico with its plain Ionic columns transpires to be a neo-classical introduction of 1806–8 by William Wilkins. The rest of the front all dates from 1701–3.

Inside the glory of Calke is that it is a house where time has stood still for more than a century. The hall hung with antlers and the adjoining bird lobby crowded with cases of stuffed animals from floor to ceiling, immediately pronounce a family whose interests have been centred in natural history. On the first floor a vast two-storey saloon occupies the whole centre of the house. Off this opens one of the most remarkable rooms to be found in any English country house, a Victorian drawing room which not only recalls the cluttered look of Victorian photographs with chairs, sofas and tables filling every available inch of floor space, and every table and surface

covered with ornaments, but which is still pristine in colour. Victorian photographs of such rooms are always in black and white or sepia and tend to look dark, overwhelmed by rich materials, heavy wallpapers and stained woodwork. The impression is of rooms dominated by mahogany or oak furniture, wallpapers with the tone of Spanish leather, landscapes lost beneath coats of varnish and velvet upholstery or leather armchairs.

The drawing room at Calke is a revelation. The colours are light and brilliant – fresh yellow and gold wallpaper, a warm pink carpet, a set of bright yellow damask sofas and chairs, and other chairs embroidered with pink and red flowers on a pink background. All the ornaments are equally colourful – white biscuit statues, brightly-tinted porcelain, gilt picture frames glistening in the light.

From the saloon we began a tour through the back passages. Room after room was filled with the accumulations of the centuries – many of them were perhaps junk rooms but rooms where nothing had ever been thrown away, where every electric light, as well as every oil lamp ever used by the family, seemed to be preserved. The greatest marvel of all was the state bed covered with brilliantly coloured Chinese silk, dating from the late eighteenth century. The fabrics had been stored in boxes ever since so they are all in perfect condition.

Offices and outbuildings are equally untouched. In the large timber stores, Gervase Jackson Stops wrote in his report for the National Trust, were " . . . templates and tools hanging from every hook, drawers filled with hinges and drawer-handles, a scene so old-fashioned that it could almost be a scene from Diderot's *Encyclopédie*".

Calke, with all its contents, its park and enough land to endow it, had been offered by the owner, Mr Henry Harpur-Crewe, to the nation in settlement of some £8 million of Capital Transfer Tax. The hope was that the Government would accept the whole package and hand it to the National Trust. After lengthy negotiations the Treasury finally agreed to accept the house, its contents and its immediate surrounding parkland, but not the endowment, whether

OPPOSITE: The baroque saloon at Calke with the neo-classical ceiling, added in 1841.
OVERLEAF: The Victorian drawing room at Calke. Curtains, chaircovers, wallpapers protected from the light for over a century, retain all their original colour.

in the form of outlying land, or capital raised from the sale of land. Without this endowment the National Trust could not accept the house.

Yet in the twenty-five years following the end of the Second World War, the system of accepting great houses in lieu of death duties had brought the National Trust many of its finest country houses. It is difficult to remember now that the National Trust's country house scheme had only begun in 1936, and in 1939 it still had only one great house, Blickling in Norfolk. Yet after the war a whole succession of great houses had come to the National Trust through the in-lieu procedures. They included many of its finest properties – Cothele, Penrhyn, Farnborough, Melford, Shugborough, Beningbrough, Hardwick, Ickworth, Saltram, Sissinghurst and Sudbury. Just imagine the loss to the nation's heritage if these houses had not been saved and transferred to the National Trust. Yet since the Government's acceptance of Cragside in Northumberland in 1977, not one great English country house had come up through the in-lieu procedures. In Scotland, one house, Brodie Castle had been accepted in 1978.

In the meantime, we had witnessed the break up of a series of great country house collections: Hever Castle and Godmersham Park in 1982, and before that Downton Castle in Shropshire, Serlby Hall in Nottinghamshire, North Mimms in Hertfordshire and Shottesham Park in Norfolk.

One of the problems in making the case for Calke Abbey was that only a handful of people had ever seen it, and its history had never been written. However, in the summer of 1983, Mr Harpur-Crewe agreed to a series of articles in *Country Life*. Alex Starkey spent a week photographing the house in September; the photographs were rushed through and suddenly we had a marvellous and quite comprehensive record of the house. By great good fortune Howard Colvin, author of the classic *Dictionary of British Architects*, had been piecing together the history of Calke from documents in the house and agreed to write three scholarly articles in a very short time. I was able to alter the country house schedule of *Country Life* so they could be published immediately; the first article appeared on 20 October and the two others in the following two weeks. At last the story, and fascination, of Calke was paraded for all to see. But all the time the future of the house was becoming gloomier. Howard Colvin had concluded his articles with the words: "Unless fiscal policy can be induced to bow to public opinion, these articles are likely to be Calke's obituary and these photographs its principal record."

Calke Abbey was caught in a Catch 22 situation which Colin Amery well summarized in the *Financial Times* on 14 November: "The Treasury's intransigence means that although the Government accepts the value to the National Heritage of this house at the same time it is refusing to make it possible for it to be supported. What a bizarre situation when we struggle to ensure the preservation of an historical continuity on one hand and refuse to allow flexible decision making to provide the means for it on the house."

The immediate need was to mobilize public opinion and we set out to do this through a SAVE lightning leaflet *This magical house must be saved intact. Now*! which we issued on 21 November. Large numbers were sent to Members of Parliament and to Peers as well as to Save supporters encouraging them to write to the Chancellor of the Exchequer and the Secretary of State for the Environment championing Calke's cause. Meanwhile Lord Gibson launched a correspondence in *The Times* on 21 November forcefully setting out the National Trust's desire to save the house. A few days later *The Times* published a letter from a Conservative MP challenging Lord Gibson's plea and concluding: "We have not heard enough about other ways of securing the future of the Calke Abbey." The day before there had been another rebuff at Question Time in the House of Commons when Mr. Neil Macfarlane, the Under Secretary of State at the Department of the Environment dealing with historic buildings matters, had restated that the Government would not accept the endowment land in lieu of tax. He also cast doubts as to whether the National Heritage Memorial Fund would help. "The Trustees of the Fund," he said, "did not consider Calke was of such a high priority as other cases then before them." After this *Times* correspondence, opinion swung unanimously in favour of Calke. No-one was fiercer than James Lees-Milne, former historic buildings adviser to the National Trust. On 3 December he wrote: "Calke is admittedly not as important in architectural terms as, say, Belton or Kedleston. Nonetheless, I dare to guess that this most endearingly

English of squires' houses would prove to be just as popular histori-
cally and artistically as the great masterpieces.

"In our National Gallery you will find larger crowds admiring
a Stubbs' landscape than a Rubens' altarpiece. Who has the right to
declare that their taste is at fault? The Treasury apparently. And so
the Treasury is going to deprive the public of one more slice of
England's heritage."

On 9 December *The Times* published a magnificent leader
championing the cause of Calke, written with an eloquence worthy
of Evelyn Waugh's *Brideshead Revisited*. "One baronet after another
would settle into his vast estates to manage them in a benevolent and
eccentric fashion, turning his back on society beyond the demesne.
The mansion being vast, a new occupant had no need to clear the
clutter of his predecessor; he chose another room. And so the
accumulation and fossilization continued, far surpassing Erdig's or
Osborne's." The message of *The Times* was clear. "Even discount-
ing the highest flights of enthusiasm Calke Abbey is without
question worth preserving intact."

The Government, however, remained unmoved. Lord
Skelmersdale on 21 December, answering a question by Lord
Strabolgi, made play of the fact that Calke was "so far little known"
and "neither the finest nor, as yet anyway, the best loved" of
England's fine heritage of important buildings. He placed some
hope on a meeting called by Lord Charteris on 10 January 1984.
Over Christmas and the New Year – when papers are thirsty for
news – the coverage of Calke grew and grew: a long piece on
Channel Four News just before Christmas, prominent feature
articles in the *Guardian*, *The Times* and *The New Standard*.

Suddenly the outlook began to brighten. Lord Montagu,
Chairman of the new Historic Buildings and Monuments Commission was taking an interest and the Heritage Fund issued a press
release announcing their meeting boldly entitled "Calke Abbey –
Towards a solution". The statement issued immediately after this
meeting on 10 January was even more encouraging. The Department of the Environment had agreed to look again at the extent of
'heritage land' surrounding the house which they might accept in
lieu of capital tax "with a view to seeing whether new facts justify
extending the boundary". The National Trust, with the help of

anonymous benefactors, was also hoping to come forward with a financial contribution, and the Harpur-Crewe trustees were examining ways in which they could help to bridge the gap.

For two months everything went silent. We knew a decision was likely to be announced about the middle of March, and there was little we could do but wait. Then on 4 March, came a counter-attack in *The Sunday Times* decrying Calke Abbey, by Lord Vaizey, a member of the Parliamentary Heritage Group. In bold print the article announced: "I should be very sorry if it were pulled down. But much of the stuff at Calke is junk." Lord Vaizey talked of: " . . . skiploads of junk . . . junk of two centuries, never sorted out by a new wife, just piled up and rarely if ever cleaned. Is this what is meant by heritage?"

Next Sunday the reply was swift and sure – in the form of a letter by Howard Colvin. In the course of a brief visit to Calke, he observed, Lord Vaizey would not have had the opportunity to look closely at these "skiploads of junk". Had he done so, Howard Colvin continued, " . . . he might have written less disparagingly about a collection which includes Bronze Age swords, silver by Paul Lamerie, eighteenth-century Chinese silk hangings in mint condition, an autograph musical score by Haydn, trophies of the battle of Trafalgar, the library of a famous Egyptologist, and paintings not all "indifferent", by Landseer, Lawrence, Linnell, Ruysdael, Ferneley, Sartorius and Tilly Kettle."

By this time, however, a decision one way or other, must have been taken. From the few soundings we could take, it seemed likely to be favourable. So we stayed silent. However, the news nonetheless came in an unexpectedly dramatic way. On Tuesday 13 March the new Chancellor, Mr. Nigel Lawson, in his first Budget speech, announced the Government was providing the National Heritage Memorial Fund with additional finance to save Calke Abbey. I heard the news from Simon Jenkins who, as political editor of *The Economist*, had been listening to the speech in the House of Commons. "It was quite amazing," he reported. "Early on in his speech the Chancellor said he had no public expenditure announcements to make – bar one. Calke Abbey. It's quite unprecedented for the Chancellor to single out a particular building in this way. Bravo!"

GARDENS

"YOU CAN'T PRESERVE GARDENS. They're ephemeral. I have just been reading Roy Strong's new book, *The Renaissance Garden in England*. Every one of those Elizabethan and Jacobean gardens, as he says, has vanished completely." So spoke a senior civil servant in the Department of the Environment, with whom I was crossing swords early in 1979, about the need for some form of official protection for gardens on the lines of that was accorded to buildings. Virtually every country in Europe makes provision for the protection of sites as well as monuments which ensures that a number of gardens and parks are protected. In Britain it is only archaeological sites and the environs of ancient monuments that receive any such protection. Some county councils, notably Staffordshire, have taken a commendable initiative in declaring important gardens such as Biddulph Grange as conservation areas but the Department of the Environment's only response has been to issue a governessy circular to planning authorities discouraging this practice on the grounds that conservation area controls were suitable only for buildings.

The point the civil servants would not grasp – and I fear still will not – is that we are not seeking to impose an obligation on owners to maintain a garden or in some way to stop the clock. This is obviously an impossibility when plants are constantly changing and being renewed. What we are seeking is simply to give some initial recognition to a garden as an entity, and to protect it from radical external change such as road building or partition for development.

OPPOSITE: The view west from Lord Leverhulme's garden at Rivington, Lancashire. Thomas Mawson's garden structures superbly match the mood of this rugged landscape.

However, gardens are less ephemeral than might appear. Some of the most exciting discoveries I have made have been of lost gardens, principally while I was working on a conservation section for the Victoria and Albert Museum Exhibition "The Garden", held in the summer of 1979. While an abandoned building, however beautiful, is inevitably an agonizing sight, with a garden the discovery that anything at all remains immensely exhilarating. For while a house may be completely razed to the ground and the site levelled so there is virtually no trace of its existence, a garden is very rarely systematically destroyed unless it is built over. Usually it is simply left to run wild becoming increasingly entangled in undergrowth.

"The formal gardens of sixteenth- and seventeenth-century England," Roy Strong wrote with characteristic incisiveness in *The Renaissance Garden in England*, "are a totally lost art form." He had dedicated his book to "all those gardens destroyed by Capability Brown and his successors". In his book, Roy Strong shows that even those few gardens thought to survive from the Elizabethan and Jacobean periods, like Packwood in Warwickshire, were in fact recreations, or at least wholesale replantings, of the nineteenth century.

While working on the exhibition, and preparing the accompanying SAVE report *Elysian Gardens,* it emerged there was one class of gardens which had escaped remodelling according to the naturalistic tastes of the second half of the eighteenth century – the gardens of country houses which had been demolished in the late seventeenth or eighteenth century and never replaced. Although these gardens were presumably abandoned at the time of demolition (or even before), in many cases substantial earthworks remain and provide fascinating first hand evidence of garden design in the sixteenth and seventeenth century.

The first systematic study of lost gardens was made by Christopher Taylor while working on the Northamptonshire volumes of the Royal Commission on Historical Monuments. He calculated that some fifty such 'lost' gardens survived in the county and on this basis surmised that as many as 2000 might exist in England as a whole. The identification and study of these gardens had been largely based initially on a unique series of aerial photographs, taken over thirty years, by Professor J.K.S. St Joseph, the director of aerial photography at Cambridge University. Certain types of light and weather conditions are wonderfully effective in showing up the traces of lost gardens. For example, the long shadows cast by a low sun on clear winter days can pick out not only features such as terraces and parterres, but even the outlines of paths and flower beds. Similarly, during summer droughts the pattern of parterres and other ornamental features subsequently grassed over can show up clearly through the turf.

Armed with Professor St. Joseph's photographs and the Royal Commission volumes I set out for Northamptonshire to visit some of these gardens and more particularly to see whether it was possible to date them and assign them a place in the development of garden design. Here, Northamptonshire was of special interest as it was very much a courtiers' county in the Elizabethan and Jacobean periods and, as Roy Strong had shown, the major innovations in garden design had taken place in court circles.

THREE NORTHAMPTONSHIRE LOST GARDENS

The first garden I visited was Holdenby. The great house built by Elizabeth's Lord Chancellor, Sir Christopher Hatton, c.1570–83 had been almost entirely demolished during the Commonwealth: what remained had been incorporated into a new house of the 1870s and 1880s. The two arched gateways of Hatton's great house, standing isolated in a field, had long been thought of as the lone survivors of his work. But in Professor St. Joseph's photograph taken in January 1975, a low sun had picked out the stepped terraces on either side of the former knot garden, each rising about a metre. These corresponded exactly with terraces shown on a 1580 survey of the house and gardens where they were marked as rosaries. A rosary was a fascinating feature at this date, and amidst the arbors, orchards and knots usually found on Elizabethan plans, was evidence of an extensive formal specialized flower garden.

There are also significant Elizabethan garden remains close to Sir Thomas Tresham's New Bield at Lyveden in the north-east of the county. Tresham, who became a fervent Catholic convert in

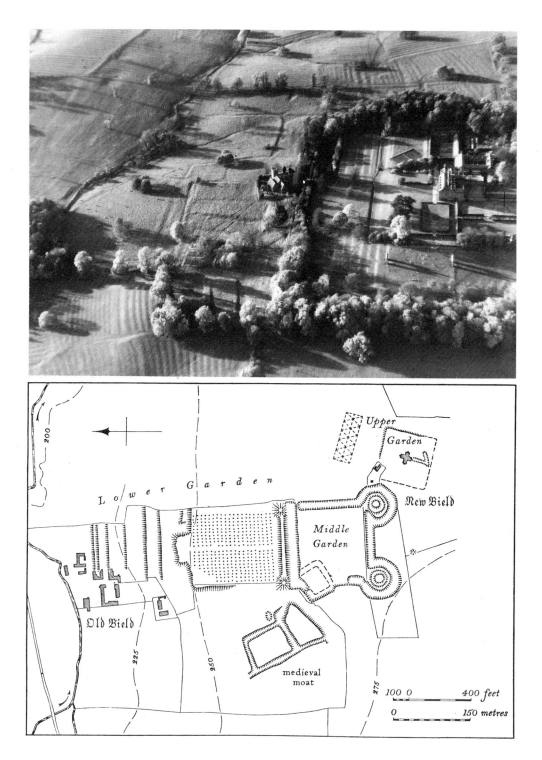

1580, gave architectural expression to his faith through a series of extraordinary buildings notably the triangular Lodge at Rushton, an allegory on the Trinity. New Bield, begun in the 1590s, is in the form of a Greek cross and was left unfinished at Tresham's death in 1605. Correspondence indicates that work on the garden was going ahead at the same time and the most notable element to survive is the so-called Middle Garden. This consists of a square enclosed on three sides by a moat with projecting circular bastions at the southern corners. On each of these is a mount ascended by an encircling path. Beyond the moat, at the north end, a large bank acts both as a dam and as an elevated terrace overlooking the garden with square stepped mounts at either end.

Before the Middle Garden had been studied and recognized for what it was this type of garden had only been known from descriptions. Sir Henry Fanshawe had laid out such a garden at Ware Park in Hertfordshire which he inherited in 1601 and John Chamberlain, five years later wrote of "rampars, bulwarkes, counterscarpes, and all other appertenances, so that when yt is finished, yt is like to prove an invincible peece of work". Verses by Andrew Marvell on the gardens laid out by Sir Thomas Fairfax at Appleton House in Yorkshire note similar features:

> *His warlike studies would not cease;*
> *But laid these Gardens out in sport,*
> *In the just Figure of a Fort.*

From Lyveden I drove north to Wakerley, very close to the border with Rutland. Here again Professor St. Joseph's photographs had picked out not only terraces but the outline of the paths and parterres of a lost garden. Walking across the field in which the garden now lies, it was surprising how marked the changes of level between the terraces still were. The garden was not particularly large and at first sight seemed no more than a fairly typical formal

OPPOSITE ABOVE: Aerial view of Holdenby Hall, Northamptonshire. The house is visible on the right, and just below on either side, the stepped terraces of the Elizabethan garden are picked out by the sunlight. BELOW: Plan of the Middle Garden at Lyveden, New Bield, Northamptonshire. A rare example of a garden laid out on a fortress plan, dating from the 1590s. The plan shows the site of the encircling moat, the projecting bastions with mounts and the raised terrace at the north end.

garden of a small manor house of the Restoration period. Yet its history, on further examination, suggested it was probably pre-Civil War in date and thus important evidence of a phase and type of gardening previously known only in engravings or glimpsed in the background of portraits.

In the early seventeenth century the house had belonged to Sir Edward Griffin of Dingley (the Dingley described in the last chapter) but in 1618 had been sold to Sir Richard Cecil of Colly-weston, second son of the First Earl of Exeter and twice MP for Peterborough. Though he had immediately leased it, the inventory made at his death noted "one leaden cistern with spouts and other things" in the garden.

The aerial photographs show the parterre was not only symmetrical but laid out on the axis of the centre of the east front. This more monumental treatment with house and garden conceived in unison is usually associated with two gardens of the 1630s – Rycote in Oxfordshire and Durdans in Surrey, both overlooked by terraces like Wakerley. As Cecil died in 1633, Wakerley could therefore precede these two. A parallel for the circular parterre at Wakerley can also be drawn with Sir John Danvers's garden at Chelsea begun in 1622 and regarded by the antiquary John Aubrey as the first Italian garden in England.

The most spectacular of these lost gardens in Northamptonshire is undoubtedly Harrington, near Kettering. The remains of the layout are just visible over a low stone wall on the edge of the road that goes through the village. The garden is now a large field grazed by cattle. Though the view from the top is impressive the house stood at the bottom of the slope – so originally you would have walked up the terraces from the house. The spectacular way in which these terraces ascend the hillside is again best shown in Professor St. Joseph's photographs, but they are also clearly visible from the ground. Beginning from the rough patch of ground marking the site of the house, the first terrace is flat, though the indentations of straight, broad paths can be seen: the second terrace

OPPOSITE ABOVE: Wakerley, Northamptonshire. In this aerial view the L-shaped terraces of the 17th-century formal garden are clearly visible. BELOW: Aerial view of Harrington, Northamptonshire. The great stepped terraces of the baroque garden, dating from *c.* 1700, are clearly visible.

recedes in baroque fashion in a concave curve. The third contains a large trapezoidal pond 4¾ feet deep with a spring on the upper side. "Tredding by cattle along the edges," the Royal Commission volume notes, "has exposed a layer of blue clay about 5cm thick, which is presumably the original lining of the pond put in to retain the water." The fourth terrace has two square depressions which were probably once small ponds or even fountains. Two paths cut through the terraces, and converge in pincer fashion on the upper-most terrace. Here there is a lozenge-shaped depression, again probably a pond, which would presumably have contained some feature such as a statue to terminate the vista from the house.

Though Harrington is sometimes loosely referred to as an Elizabethan garden it is clear it is a highly sophisticated baroque piece of design, an English counterpart albeit on a more modest scale than the baroque gardens on the hillsides of Frascati near Rome. Baroque, is the visual theme of a garden designed to be taken in at a glance and baroque, the use of converging diagonals, concave curves and trapezoids instead of simple squares and rectangles. This fits with the written visual evidence for Harrington must have been laid out between 1675 and 1712. Bridges, writing about 1720, states that the gardens were laid out by "the present Earl, the 3rd Earl of Dysart, who succeeded in 1675", while Morton in his *Natural History of Northamptonshire* (1712) wrote that "for a descent of Garden Walks there is nothing so remarkable with us as that of the Walks at Harrington."

EASTON LODGE

The Northamptonshire lost gardens were mostly abandoned some two or three hundred years ago but among the most exciting lost gardens I have found have been late Victorian or Edwardian gardens, sometimes completely abandoned, sometimes just forgotten. It was on such a quest that I set off on a Saturday morning in the spring of 1979 with John and Eileen Harris and Anne, my wife, in search of gardens both lost and preserved, in Hertfordshire and Essex. We spent a fascinating half hour at Fanhams, a Japanese garden of the early 1900s, beautifully tended by the Association of Building Societies that used the house. Later in the day we found just outside

Ware in the middle of a new housing development, an almost intact mid-eighteenth-century shell grotto. This was built in the 1770s for John Scott of Millbrook House. It was entangled in shrubs and undergrowth and announced unexpectedly by a street sign proclaiming "The Grotto – cul-de-sac". We scrambled in and found, with the help of a ladder standing conveniently in position, that we could descent through the dome, or oculus, in the roof. There, remarkably intact was all the original shellwork laid in ornamental patterns, mixed with spar and other semi-precious stones. The local authority had acquired the grotto to preserve it and was shortly to carry out repairs.

The highlight of the trip came at the end of the day when we went to see if anything remained of the Countess of Warwick's garden at Easton Lodge in Essex. The gardens had been superbly photographed by *Country Life* for an article in 1907 and appeared in Christopher Hussey's and Gertrude Jekyll's folio volume *Garden Ornament* but the house had been demolished and as far as we could ascertain the garden had completely vanished. In the old photographs it looked a perfect combination of formal architectural layout softened by lush exuberant planting. The most striking features were a wonderful sunken garden with a balustraded pool, domed wooden pergolas on a monumental scale and a Japanese tea house standing in pristine condition by a lake.

According to Avray Tipping in his *Country Life* article of 1907, the gardens had been laid out in 1902 to the designs of Harold Peto who had collected the antique statues which adorned the garden at judicious points. Peto was a brilliant garden designer, and surprisingly still awaits a biographer, but his gardens both in England and on the French Riviera were unusually well recorded at the time. More than anyone after him, I think, he mastered the art of blending architecture, sculpture and planting in a totally unselfconscious way. So often sculpture looks posed or contrived in a garden and architectural features, whether pavilions or balustrades, look raw for several years or more. But Peto clearly knew which plants would prosper and provide the right effects and was sufficiently steeped in arts and crafts building traditions to ensure that buildings looked in place. So he created gardens that, in retrospect, seem mature and at their prime almost instantly.

ABOVE: The sunken garden at Easton Lodge, Essex in the 1900s. Designed by Harold Peto for the Countess of Warwick, Edward VII's 'Darling Daisy'. OPPOSITE: The remains of the sunken garden at Easton in 1979 discovered beneath thick undergrowth. The house was demolished soon after the Second World War.

Easton, Tipping wrote, "was five years ago deplorably deficient in pleasant garden surroundings, those in existence consisting of very moderate sized squares of grass cut up with commonplace flower bed arrangements." Part of the park was taken in, and by 1907 the pergolas of "sixteenth-century type" were "already wreathed and bowered with creepers". Beyond was the sunk Garden of Ham Hill stone with a "balustraded pool, akin to the original one at Montacute, but on a larger scale, as it takes the form of a canal over 100 foot in length, which in summer is literally ablaze with various coloured waterlilies." These waterlilies, chosen by Peto, had flourished beyond all expectation in the cold climate of Essex, due it was thought to the heat radiating from the stone flagging. The Countess of Warwick – Edward VII's "Darling Daisy"

– was an avid gardener and had founded a college for training
women in gardening. At Easton she had employed some seventy
Salvation Army waifs as well as all available local labour in the
immense work of earthmoving.

The gardens at Easton Lodge, I later learnt from Mrs Spurrier,
a granddaughter of the Countess of Warwick, had flourished in
splendid maturity until the second world war. Lady Warwick, who
died in 1938, is commemorated in a very Edwardian-looking bust in
Little Easton Church. There had been a fire in the house in 1918,
causing extensive damage, but this had been repaired. The real
tragedy began, Mrs Spurrier wrote, "in 1942 when the American
Army Air Force built a bomber base on the deer park which involved
the destruction of something like 12,000 trees." After the war the
house was considered to have been so neglected during requisition-
ing that there was no alternative to demolition.

The *Country Life* article has shown a number of half-timbered
estate cottages built, it appeared, for the large house parties the

Countess held, rather like the "village" the Astors added to Hever, and these still survived. We inquired about the garden and were pointed to some shrubs. At first these looked impenetrable but we ducked low under the bushes and by degrees pushed our way forward. Here and there were remains of formal planting and soon we came to a long hedge. In a gap we found some stone steps and there before us, enshrouded in brambles and visible only because the leaves were hardly on the branches, was the balustraded pool. We walked round and found it complete almost in its entirety apart from a few missing sections of balustrade. Here indeed was evidence of how the bones of a garden could survive complete abandonment for 40 years. Beneath dense undergrowth Petro's garden layout remained – it had simply run wild and been forgotten.

COPPED HALL

Some five years earlier I stumbled inadvertently on another lost Edwardian garden, this time at Copped Hall near Epping in Essex. I was collecting material for articles in *Country Life* on country house parks threatened by road proposals and had heard that Copped Hall would be affected. The house was no more than a gutted shell, but the walls were surprisingly intact, and have remained so, and could still be rebuilt internally and be lived in again. Immediately beside the house was a pigsty with a number of very large and boisterous looking pigs running free and charging back and forth so that not a blade of grass could be seen, giving Copped the air of being George Orwell's *Animal Farm* come to life.

The house, I learnt later, had been built about 1753 for a Tory MP, John Conyers, by John Sanderson, an architect involved in the building of a number of handsome, if fairly conventional, Palladian houses. Here he appears to have worked under the direction of two gentlemen dabblers in architecture – Sir Roger Newdigate, whose Arbury Hall in Warwickshire is the Strawberry Hill of the Midlands, and Thomas Prowse of Wicken in Northamptonshire and Berkeley House near Frome in Somerset. Before this an Elizabethan house of great interest had stood on the site.

James Wyatt had carried out alterations in 1775–77 but when

Avray Tipping wrote about the house in *Country Life* in 1910 it had recently been extensively reworked by C.E. Kemp, a well-known designer and maker of stained glass. Kemp's interiors alas had perished in or following a disastrous fire of 1917 and as far as I knew no trace remained of the elaborate architectural gardens he had laid out behind the house. The old photographs show an overpoweringly architectural formal garden on a large scale with many balustrades and very broad gravel paths so that lawns and beds were but small incidents of colour. It was in fact the exact opposite of Easton Lodge where Peto had softened the architectural elements by planting: here everything was as neat and tidy as could be. Kemp had a love of vertical accents, placing obelisks on the balustrades and columns in the fountains. The main axis to the western garden gates was prolonged by a causeway with lower parterres on either side connected by archways underneath. But the most fantastic element was a pair of classical garden pavilions at either corner of the main terrace, executed in superb ashlar masonry. They were a wonderful example of what the Danes called *stilvorring* or stylistic confusion – as Tipping points out, a florid Palladianism with touches of Jacobean and swags and drops of sculptured fruit in the manner of Wren.

When I walked round the ruined shell of the house I expected to find all trace of the garden vanished: the balustrades and obelisks vandalized or taken away long ago by dealers. But though the undergrowth was thick, it was fortunately only February and there, through the saplings and brambles I spotted one of the temples – the doors and windows gone but otherwise intact. A little further was the causeway with the arched bridges beneath – once again in fact the bones of the garden had survived the long abandonment, and given the will, it could be restored – even if in simplified fashion.

BIDDULPH GRANGE

One of the most powerful and bewitching single black-and-white photographs of a garden ever published is a picture of the Chinese

OVERLEAF: *Country Life* view of the Edwardian formal gardens at Copped Hall, Epping in 1905. The twin pavilions and terraces survive though balustrades, urns and obelisks have long since disappeared.

Garden at Biddulph Grange in Staffordshire. It was published in *Country Life* in 1905 and we had then used it as a large blow-up in the Country House Exhibition at the Victoria and Albert in 1974. It is one of those photographs which captivates because it is hard to believe that even in 1905 such a place existed. So it was all the more exciting to find that the garden still survives, ailing but substantially intact.

Today Biddulph Grange is an orthopaedic hospital and the gardens are only open to the public once a year. Yet in the nineteenth century they were very much on show: the *Gardeners' Chronicle* of 25 May 1862 states that the public were admitted every Monday from May to September, and by ticket purchased in advance, every Friday throughout the year, except Good Friday. Foreigners and those who had travelled from afar were allowed in on other days but no one was ever admitted on Sundays.

The creator of this garden was James Bateman (1811–97) who had been brought up nearby at Knypersley Hall. While very young he had displayed great interest in tropical plants and according to the 1905 *Country Life* article "before he took his degree at Oxford in 1834 he had sent out collectors to the West Indies to bring home plants for cultivation which were described in Loudon's *Gardeners' Magazine*. From Mexico and Guatemala also he procured many rare and beautiful orchids." In 1837 he began his great work on the orchidaceae of these countries, which was published in 1843 in atlas folio with large colour plates in a limited edition of one hundred copies.

Before James Bateman began work the site was a swampy moor but from about 1845 onwards he completely transformed it creating "a variety of miniature hills and dales, nooks and recesses, to secure shelter and exposure, sun and shade, lake and stream, suitable to a great variety of plants." Edward Kemp in the *Gardeners' Chronicle* in 1856 describes how Mr. and Mrs. Bateman found "their chief occupation and amusement in personally directing the progress of the various works". But after the second series of articles in the *Gardeners' Chronicle* in 1862 James Bateman wrote a letter to the

OPPOSITE: The Chinese Garden at Biddulph Grange, Staffordshire in 1900. One of the most exotic and colourful of all Victorian gardens.

OPPOSITE: Biddulph Grange. The entrance to China in 1979. The Pavilion was finally destroyed by vandals in 1983. ABOVE: Biddulph Grange. An Egyptian temple in clipped yew, still surviving intact.

editor to give credit to his friend, the painter Edward Cooke "to whose every-ready pencil and inexhaustible invention my gardens, I am well aware, owe their chief attractions". Cooke was a great authority on ferns, and his successive London homes, both called the Ferns, had ferneries. As a marine painter he had developed a fascination for rocks and coasts which led him into rock gardening on a large scale – which he practiced first in William Wells' garden at Redleaf, Surrey.

Perplexingly, both Knypersley and Biddulph Grange were put up for sale in 1871, just 29 years after Bateman had acquired Biddulph but the extensive sale particulars are an excellent check list of the garden's main features at its moment of maximum extent – with Chinese, Egyptian, and Italian Gardens, "the valuable collection of Araucarias (perhaps the finest in England)", the great Wellingtonia Avenue, the Pinetum, the Glen and the Stumpery being but the principal highlights.

Bateman's house was largely rebuilt in 1897 after a fire, and quite a number of the features around the house – the camellia and rhododendron houses, the dahlia walk and Mrs Bateman's garden (which Kemp said offered "every sort of facility for lady gardening") had gone. When I first went to Biddulph in August 1978 I had expected to find the gardens ragged but the initial view from the garden terrace down to a miniature lake showed everything to be in good condition: plenty of well bedded young rhododendrons, trim lawns and paths amongst the outcrops of rock. With a limited budget the hospital was achieving a remarkable amount. But the main features of Bateman's garden are ingeniously hidden. Impatient to reach the Chinese garden we walked round behind the lake to a long walk, skirting the edge of the grounds through the Pinetum. Here Kemp described how Bateman had clustered various species of conifers on different mounds so their silhouettes, even when young, would always be seen against the sky.

"The Chinese Garden," Kemp wrote, "like China itself is very difficult of access and strangers will sometimes wander for hours without finding either of the two very narrow entrances." Today the Chinese garden is still equally well concealed, and the experience of entering this secret enclosure is still magical. Kemp and every writer since has observed how it is the willow pattern plate brought to life. The bridge is still there, though rebuilt in simpler form since the *Country Life* photograph, but what startled us most in 1978 was the brilliant colouring of the temple beyond. Here Bateman had cultivated Chinese plants and in the right season the trees and shrubs are ablaze with colour so red leaves and red woodwork dominate the garden. The Chinese garden was still incomplete when Kemp wrote about Biddulph in 1856 and three years later Cooke noted in his diary ". . . busy all day in garden at work at Joss House, Chinese Temple etc and painting and trying experiments." By 1862 other features included a great frog couchant, sundry Chinese monstrosities including a huge gilt bull, which still survives, modelled on the spot by the sculptor Waterhouse Hawkins. All around there are glimpses of ruined walls, dilapidated towers and doorways suggestive of the Great Wall of China.

At the eastern end of the Chinese garden was a root garden known as The Stumpery. This consisted of old roots and rugged stumps of trees piled ten or twelve feet high on either side of a twisting walk. The Stumpery was arranged to form rustic arches in parts. Elsewhere these receded to allow room for "little gatherings of choice herbaceous plants, bulbs or miniature shrubs".

Beyond the Chinese garden the walk through the Pinetum is terminated by a black and white Cheshire Cottage. From here you turn at right angles and enter what is now a dingy and damp passage to emerge wholly unexpectedly in Bateman's final *tour de force*, the Egyptian Temple created out of clipped yew.

Over the centuries topiary has been formed into garden rooms of all shapes and sizes, most memorably perhaps in the long Homeric walls climbing the hillside at Rous Lench in Worcestershire. It was Bateman's and Cooke's genius to conceive how suited topiary was to the solid geometry of Egyptian temple architecture with its sheer massive walls devoid of all windows. The topiary in Bateman's garden is quite simply a series of rectangles stepped back with the pyramid at the top. Yet simply by the addition of an Egyptian doorhead and a pair of sphinxes a brilliant Egyptian effect is achieved. All that seems surprising today, in the century of Tutenkhamun, is that Biddulph has not had more imitators. Though a little ragged in places the walls of the temple still retain their bulk and outline. Biddulph is yet another example of the way garden features can survive both vicissitudes and passing time.

When I went to Biddulph again in 1979, the outlook was hopeful: the Chinese Temple was rather crudely protected behind a makeshift barbed wire barricade, but a Restoration Association was being formed to take a lease on the gardens and begin restoration. Since then the position has gone from bad to worse, due quite simply to the machinations of bureaucracy. The Restoration Association had been negotiating with the Staffordshire Area Health Authority but under the second round of National Health Reorganization in 1982, this authority was to be abolished, and its responsibilities transferred to the new North Staffordshire Area Health Authority. The outgoing authority was unwilling to bind its successor, but in 1983 negotiations were resumed on a friendly basis. By this time the new authority was carrying out a review of hospital provision in its area and published a consultative paper proposing the closure of Biddulph within five to seven years.

The Charity Commissioners, however, will not grant the Restoration Association charitable status if the lease is likely to be a maximum of seven years: but this is all the health authority will offer as it does not wish to be in the position of selling the estate with "a sitting tenant" – though to some purchasers the existence of a trust looking after the gardens might be an attraction. All this might be merely amusing, but for what has happened to the garden in the meantime. One of the first aims of the Restoration Association was to erect a security fence to keep out vandals; this has not been done, and in 1983 the wonderfully exotic and colourful Chinese Temple illustrated here was largely wrecked by vandals. As I write the Joss House is under attack.

If there had been some official form of protection for gardens, Biddulph undoubtedly would have been given the highest rating. This might have secured action in time. As it is, the Chinese Temple will in the course of time probably be reconstructed (though there are no measured drawings to work from), but this will undoubtedly cost a deal more than the straightforward repairs needed in 1979.

FRIAR PARK

It is hard to imagine that there could be anywhere a garden more exotically contrived than Biddulph Grange, but just outside Henley survives a still more fantastic garden at Friar Park. This was the creation of Sir Frank Crisp, best known as the author of two scholarly and beautifully produced volumes on *Medieval Gardens* published in 1924. There is an amusing study to be made of the late nineteenth-century fixation with friars – of which the opulent Arts and Crafts Black Friar pub by Blackfriars Bridge in London is another example. There, as at Friar Park, much is made of the merriness of the friar, but Crisp carried it to extreme lengths as he was one of those people who could not resist a pun and everywhere puns, often rather lugubrious, appear inscribed in gothic letters on the stonework.

OPPOSITE: The Matterhorn at Friar Park, Oxfordshire. This early *Country Life* colour photograph, taken *c.* 1905 shows Sir Frank Crisp's Alpine planting. The 'snowy' peak of the Matterhorn is visible top right.

But while it is easy to be dismissive of Crisp's rather heavy sense of humour, this can detract from a proper appreciation of his inventiveness as a gardener, and his ability to carry off theatrical effects on the grand scale. Crisp produced several editions of the guide book to Friar, full of quotations illuminating the different styles and types of garden he had created. Immediately inside the entrance was a notice saying "Don't keep off the grass" which he had substituted for "the grass may be walked on" so he could observe bewildered visitors wondering what they were to do, quite a number returning to ask the attendant what was meant.

For some years after Crisp's death, Friar Park was a school and the gardens run down but by great good fortune they have now found an owner with the enthusiasm and the ability to bring Crisp's gardens back to life almost in their entirety.

Today Friar Park is an Elysium – a world turned in on itself, and shaded by large mature trees, which every few hundred yards brings a spectacular surprise. First come a series of lakes stepped one above the other so that from the top they look like a continuous sheet of water. Just beneath one of the weirs between the lakes is a row of stepping stones quite out of sight from above, so from the house it looks as if anyone crossing was walking on the water. According to the 1914 edition of his guide the stepping stones had the impressions of the naked feet of a man, a woman and six children, and further away the footprints of a four-clawed animal. The suggestion, Crisp explains, was that a prehistoric man was endeavouring to protect his family from the monster by hurrying them across the water – but the monster was catching up and he had had to turn round to confront it.

From here begins the first great adventure of Friar Park, the entrance to the underground caverns, large enough to row a boat round. These were Crisp's water caves, which he dubbed the blue caves of Capri. They consisted of two main caves with long connecting passages containing "Owls, Bats, Frogs, Toadstools, Gnomes, Waterfalls, Fossil Trees, Petrified Birds' nests". The middle cave according to the 1910 guide was "beautifully illuminated by day, especially on sunny mornings, by blue glass skylights" while in the large cave was a waterfall lit by coloured lights. Visitors could go by boat in limited numbers. A footpath along the edge of the water had to serve when they came in large groups.

Just such a system of underground caves had been created by Ludwig II at Schloss Linderhof in Bavaria, which Crisp through his international gardening interests may have known.

The second great feature of Friar Park was a scaled down version of the Matterhorn created out of huge blocks of millstone grit, some 7,000 tons in all, brought by sea from Yorkshire then transported up the Thames by barge and hauled up the hill from Henley. Crisp went to great lengths to ensure his mountain matched his model, complete with the famous snowcapped peak at the top. When *Country Life* illustrated the garden in 1905 the rocks were all in place, though the garden as a whole was still unfinished, but the brilliance of Crisp's planting is caught in a number of very rare early coloured glass negatives which survive in the photograph library at *Country Life*. According to the 1905 article: "a rill of water tumbles over rocks almost from the summit . . . bell-flowers hang in flowery drifts from the rocks, and fill chinks and crevices with colour as blue as a summer sky . . . Pinks are everywhere, not in little colonies, but masses, yards across . . . soft rose, salmon, purple, crimson, and almost blood red."

Within the Matterhorn was a further series of caves, a Vine Cave, a Skeleton Cave with distorting mirrors with an optical illusion showing Mephistopheles following Marguerite from church. There was also an Illusion Cave with another set piece showing a seated Friar being electrocuted as if in a new-fangled American electric chair.

And so the garden continued, a mixture of theatrical effects anticipating the underground boat trips of Disneyland.

RIVINGTON

Friar Park is the epitome of the fantastic in gardening – Crisp sought to create what was hardly credible, tempered only by his strange and somewhat lugubrious sense of humour. Completely in contrast is the remarkable garden created by the first Viscount Leverhulme at

OVERLEAF: Another early colour view of the Matterhorn at Friar Park. Brilliantly colourful rock gardening on a colossal scale.

Rivington in Lancashire. This, too, has a fantastic element, born of the desire to remodel nature on a heroic scale. Whereas Crisp's imagination veered towards an impish childish world of friars, toy chamois, theatrical illusions and even garden gnomes (he imported these from Bavaria and they must have been among the earliest in England), Lord Lever's garden was without statues or monsters, and veered rather to the elemental – Nordic in feeling but purely architectural and without figurative allusions.

As landscape architect he chose Thomas Mawson, author of the highly influential book *The Art and Craft of Garden Making* which went through five editions from 1900. With its neat drawings and exact plans Mawson's book is an endless source of fascination but to me they rather lack sparkle or finesse – they are just a little too dry and prosaic. Mawson needed what Lutyens, Jekyll and Peto were to gain from so immensely – superb photography, principally by *Country Life*, showing their gardens at their peak in every season of the year. By comparison the photographs in Mawson's book can be lacklustre and too often taken on a dull day.

For this reason I have found visits to Mawson's gardens all the more exciting: each one has been far better than the photographs suggested, grander and more romantic in conception, and excellent in the detail – constructed of well-chosen materials beautifully handled.

Lever had been offered the Rivington estate in 1899. It lies on the edge of the Pennines with a spectacular view disappearing into the distance over the Lancashire plain. Liverpool Corporation owned a series of reservoirs on the western edge of the property, but they expressed no interest in Rivington so Lever went ahead with the purchase. But local authorities are notorious for changing their minds on such issues and in 1902 Liverpool sought to compulsorily purchase part of the estate. With the future Earl of Birkenhead as his junior counsel Lever forced Liverpool to more than double their offer, but this left him with no more than 45 acres, which Mawson was to lay out for him.

I went to Rivington in 1979 while working on the Victoria and Albert garden exhibition. We had heard from the local council that the garden, long derelict, was now in the course of restoration – a joint venture between the North West Water Authority and the

ABOVE: An archway at Rivington, Lancashire. Mawson exploited the drama of the site to brilliant effect. Every stone in every wall was cut and placed with masterly care.

National Conservation Corps. We had been sent photographs showing clearing and burning of undergrowth: by the time I arrived the work was virtually complete. Paths were open, the planting revived, and all the architectural features visible and in excellent condition. The garden consists of a series of walks linked by staircases – some open, some ascending in tunnels and emerging on spectacular terraces. The rugged stone walls have something of

ABOVE & OPPOSITE: Nordic romance at Rivington. Large irregular stone flags were used for paths and steps.

H.H. Richardson in America or even more of the National Revival style in Finland at the turn of the century. Though there are arches with voussoirs and keystones, columns with bases and capitals, the detail is deliberately simplified: balustrades consist not of urn-shaped balusters but great crossed stones. The masonry is also extremely good – it looks as if Mawson made drawings of each wall showing the exact shape and place, perhaps even texture, of every stone. Narrow fillets of stone–like Roman bricks are tellingly juxta-posed with large blocks set in uneven courses. Mawson brilliantly responded to the drama of the site, sheltering the walks in places by massive planting and suddenly providing a terrace with a spectacular view. He was also a master at paving and surfacing. Where paved areas are too large or of the wrong texture there is always a jarring note. Mawson chose his materials brilliantly, above all for the staircases which spill out in places with the drama of waterfalls.

A few months earlier I had had another taste of Mawson's

boldness in designing architectural features for gardens. I had gone to look at the garden at The Hill, Hampstead just on the western edge of Hampstead Heath. The house is now a hospital, and the garden has been crudely cut in two: the further part is now a public park. But spanning the two Mawson's handsome pergola survives – a long run of columns carrying a wooden frame, and branching in different directions. Today it is divided midway by a barbed wire fence but it survives in remarkably good condition, well planted and one of the few opportunities to see what a grand Edwardian private garden in Hampstead looked like. And the Hill proclaims another aspect of Mawson's brilliance: he responded as well to the urbanity of London as to the wildness of the Pennines. His practice flourished in both the North of England and the South, and he perceived and mastered their very different gardening traditions to a greater extent than any of his contemporaries.

KIRBY

This chapter began with an anecdote of official scepticism about the practicality of preserving historic gardens. It is perhaps fitting to end it with the story of a couple in retirement with a passion for gardens, who wanted to do something of lasting value in the way of helping restore one historic garden.

Kirby Hall in Northamptonshire is a wonderful partly-ruined house of mainly Jacobean date looked after as an Ancient Monument by the Department of the Environment. The original layout of the garden was well-documented and the couple wanted to spend a substantial capital sum, of the order of £20,000 on recreating it. The reply from the Department was polite but firm: it was impossible to accept contributions earmarked for specific monuments but if, for example, they would like to pay for a rosebush, the Department would undertake to use its best endeavours to see one was planted at the house. A little later, in May 1981 they wrote to the Minister who replied apologizing for the discouraging reply from his officials, explaining this was "because Government accounting procedures are complex and it would simply not be possible for us to guarantee to increase the level of expenditure at Kirby Hall to match your contribution". He agreed the legislation did "make provision for us to receive voluntary contributions and we should be most pleased to receive any donation and to use it to reduce the cost to the Government of the work to the gardens at Kirby Hall". Just to suggest the gift would be used for reducing Government expenditure was hurtful, even insulting, and showed that the Department was continuing to miss the point. Once again the couple replied: "We realized that the Department would not be likely to go beyond maintenance of the gardens as they are. What we had in mind was to produce a capital sum to restore the layout and planting to something like their original form – the terraces, fountain, tree plantings, etc. The capital cost of doing this might not be very high – plants and labour – though obviously needing some thousands. Once done, the maintenance costs ought not to rise unduly, and the returns in visitors might go up substantially."

Throughout this correspondence it is clear that officials had misunderstood the nature of the offer and its implications. With a new Commission for Historic Buildings and Monuments taking over buildings like Kirby on 1 April 1984, a more enterprising and enlightened attitude may emerge.

PUBLIC BUILDINGS

"MR. BINNEY, YOU REALLY HAVE gone too far this time," said the Assistant Secretary. "Definitely too far," agreed the Under Secretary. "You'll regret this." We were standing beneath the newly gilded ceiling of Inigo Jones's Banqueting Hall in Whitehall at about half past six on the evening of Friday 18 November 1977. The occasion was a reception to mark the award of the Goethe Prize to the National Trust, which brought with it a handsome cheque for some £70,000.

The cause of the chagrin of these two civil servants was a report SAVE had just issued, provocatively entitled *Glittering Palaces for Bureaucrats*, written by Kate Pugh and published in the weekly *Building Design* on 11 November. Our aim was to highlight the vast sums being spent by central and local government on new administrative offices and to show that alternative accommodation could be provided in historic buildings, usually at considerably less cost.

Evidently our message had hit a sensitive point; a press release was promptly issued by the Department of the Environment (recognition of this kind is a compliment) in which the Minister vigorously defended the Property Services Agency (PSA) from our criticisms. We noted, however, that the examples cited on PSA conversions did not include one building converted as administrative offices – New Scotland Yard or Norman Shaw North, as it is now known, being offices for MPs. But here is an interesting point: whenever a criticism is made of the work of the PSA almost

OPPOSITE: View into the newly-restored Ladies' retiring room at the Atlanta Fox in 1982. The cinema opened on Christmas Day 1929 but had been due for demolition when in 1975 it was saved by a specially formed trust.

invariably a Minister will publicly defend the Agency very soon after – at a press conference, in an after dinner speech or on some official occasion. There is no other organization in Whitehall, the Church Commissioners excepted, where those in charge unfailingly respond to any criticism and almost invariably seek to cap adverse comment of any kind.

One of the points we had made in the report was that although the PSA had £1,727 million of work in progress it had given up publishing an annual report as an economy measure. As a result it was extremely hard to elicit any detailed information about the PSA's work – either as to the buildings they were working on or the costs involved. To try and break through the wall of silence, we had written to the directors of all the PSA regions asking a series of questions. None answered. Eventually we had a single acknowledgement from the PSA headquarters – it was inappropriate for us to talk directly to the regional offices. Eventually, after much telephoning, we found one man willing to see us. Kate Pugh and I arrived some weeks later at the PSA office in Croydon – a characteristically faceless tower block – and were shown in to a very large office behind which a senior official sat at a vast desk. The significant point about this office was that apart from the desk and chairs it was completely empty. There were no books, no papers, no ornaments, no pictures on the wall; there was just this very large expensive-looking desk intended, no doubt, to convey a precise level in the official pecking order which was completely lost on us.

Our host was a past master at parrying questions. Every piece of information we wanted was not readily available or would cost too much in staff time to answer. At this time any Parliamentary question said to cost more than £50 to answer could be dismissed as requiring a disproportionate amount of resources. But eventually we elicited a remarkable fact: it was quite impossible to tell us, or indeed anyone, the cost of any particular new building. What the Agency – and Parliament – was concerned with was how much would be spent on that particular building in any one financial year. It was a question of how much should be put in the estimates and whether the estimates had been adhered to. But surely we persisted, someone, Parliament or Ministers, would want to know the eventual cost. "Ah," he said, "that is a very difficult matter. It is not possible to say how much a building will cost until five, ten or fifteen years after its completion. Bills will still be coming in, points will be at issue with the contractors, claims may be made." So we then asked if he could at least provide the annual building costs on a select number of individual buildings. This was possible, we learnt, but would take too much time. First of all it was necessary to hunt back through the computer spools and for each year there were numerous spools, and then it took further time to find the current place on the spool, and anyway computer time would never be available for such an exercise. So our request was politely declined. Our attack in the report, however, had one good effect: the next year the PSA did produce an annual report, and continued to do so for two or three years until it was quietly dropped again.

We met the PSA in a different role early in January 1982, while a SAVE team was in Gibraltar preparing a report on the fate of Gibraltar's historic buildings. Unexpectedly perhaps, Gibraltar is remarkably rich in good buildings – Mediterranean vernacular in the old town, handsome dockyard buildings and a large number of dignified, mainly military, buildings erected by engineers in what John Harris aptly termed the 'ordnance style'. We were impressed by the high standard to which the PSA maintained the buildings: the problem was that many of the better buildings, particularly in the old town, were shortly to be vacated. This was partly prompted out of a desire to concentrate personnel in the new estate at the south end of the peninsular – which was however very prone to thick sea mist – and partly because the older buildings did not conform to a Treasury document setting out a "synopsis scale of entitlements" which each grade and rank should have. Though many of the older properties in the town were extremely attractive and much sought after by people stationed in Gibraltar, they were ruled technically substandard because, for example, the hall was of the wrong size, the requisite car parking facilities were not within easy reach, or shopping had to be carried up more than a certain number of steps. Officials of the PSA were at pains to point out that "substandard" was not meant to imply the buildings were in any way in poor condition or necessarily unattractive to live in. Such is the way large sums of public money are spent to provide new accommodation which is never really needed.

The case histories described here are intended to illustrate the range of entrenched attitudes and inflexible policies that can militate to destroy a fine public building even when it is still capable of beneficial use. With the Lyceum in Liverpool, British Rail had obtained permission to demolish the building because they claimed the land was needed for a new station. In fact, the station has been built on an adjoining site. At the Jubilee Hall in Covent Garden which had become a flourishing sports hall, the Greater London Council refused to consider alternatives to demolition. With Billingsgate Fish Market, the City Corporation had never given serious consideration to retaining the market.

All these buildings were condemned as white elephants, hopelessly unsuited to modern uses. However, all have found developers willing to restore them. The most heartening story of all must be that of the Fox Cinema in Atlanta, Georgia in the States – a 5000-seat cinema extravaganza of the 1920s rescued and restored by local people, which is now flourishing throughout the year.

LYCEUM

On a beautiful May day in 1978, I found myself in the Russian town of Suzdal with a bulging wallet containing some 150 roubles, mostly in single rouble notes, and a long list of signatures to a telegram I was to send to the British Prime Minister. I had been invited to the USSR to give a talk on the unexpected subject of "Public Opinion and the Protection of Historic Monuments", at the fifth assembly of ICOMOS, the International Council on Monuments and Sites.

I was among the youngest of the speakers and my talk was the very last before the final concluding business of the congress. From session to session, I watched numbers dwindle, lulled by the predictability of most of the talks, all too many phrased in the deadening cultural jargon of Unesco meetings. "Don't worry," a member of the Norwegian delegation assured me. "By the time you give your talk, with this beautiful weather there will be no-one left in the conference hall." That might sound a relief but on this occasion it was a matter of some concern for I had decided that the best way to end my talk was with a positive appeal to the audience to

ABOVE: Thomas Harrison's Greek Revival Lyceum in Liverpool in 1978. Consent to demolish had been granted seven years earlier but the campaign for a reprieve was gathering formidable momentum.

unite together in one simple straightforward piece of action – and save one endangered building. After all the generalities, all the broadly phrased recommendations, I hoped this would be invigorating and that the audience might respond to the challenge, which was difficult to make as most were listening to translations through earphones. My first worry was the building I had chosen, Thomas Harrison's marvellous Lyceum in Liverpool which was imminently to be demolished for a British Rail inspired property development. Lyceum was a good name, easily translated, and the noble entrance front of which I was going to show a slide would not have looked second rate beside neoclassical buildings in Naples, Berlin or Helsinki. But who would have heard the name of Thomas Harrison? Liverpool, though it was known as a great port all over the globe, was not an historic town in the sense understood by most of the delegates, charged with the care of many of the world's most beautiful ancient cities. Nor could I hope for a change in the weather to lure people back from the forty superb churches in Suzdal where we were staying. Every ICOMOS conference, I had been told by the Chairman of the UK delegation, the Duke of Grafton, had always had perfect weather from beginning to end.

By good luck I was saved by a growing trickle of people coming back to get a seat for the final session of the conference, so when I came to make my appeal for every member of the audience to pay one rouble to sign a telegram to the British Prime Minister, Mr Callaghan, asking him to secure a reprieve for the Lyceum, the auditorium was nearly half full.

Thanks to the help of John Morris, Director of the National Trust in New South Wales, I collected 150 signatures in two hours but then the dreadful problem dawned on me: how to send the telegram. Even if I had written out all the names in block letters the Russian hotel clerk would hardly be able to take an English telegram of this length, while to a post office official the English alphabet would presumably be incomprehensible. The same thought had obviously occurred to others. "Where is the party to be?" I was repeatedly asked in gently insidious tones. Nor, I thought, could I go to the British Embassy, given its obvious request for political action. Luckily John Morris had the idea of taking the list to the Australian Embassy and kindly spent the best part of the day with the telex operator preparing it all.

Why did I think such a technique would work? I had been given the idea by some literature I had once bought at the Musée Horta in Brussels. When Victor Horta's art nouveau masterpiece the Maison du Peuple in Brussels had been threatened with demolition, its champions had marshalled a petition of all the great names in architecture round the world, entreating the city fathers for a reprieve. It had not worked then but that was in the full flood of the philistinism of early 1960s: in 1978 there seemed a better chance that such a collection of signatories would make an impact. Perhaps I was over optimistic. It was not until many weeks and many letters later that I received a one sentence acknowledgement from a junior official in the Department of the Environment acknowledging the telegram from Moscow from myself and distinguished signatories. On the other hand, when I brazenly approached Mr Callaghan at a reception a few years later, he warmly recalled the incident.

The telegram did two things – it was a boost to SAVE's efforts and an encouragement to the campaign in Liverpool which until then had met a complete stonewall from local politicians. From this moment the campaign went from strength to strength – largely based on the tireless enthusiasm of Florence Gerstwyn who organized an endless series of rallies, posters, handbills and petitions. Lyceum souvenirs abounded, from the simplest buttonhole badges consisting of small pieces of cardboard with a dusty zerox of the Lyceum portico attached by a safety pin, to an endless series of Lyceum cakes – with the portico in white icing. Liverpudlians have the best sense of humour in Britain so much of the campaign literature was extremely amusing, not to say outrageous.

It also became increasingly clear that we were fighting for a building of exceptional quality. In a lightning SAVE leaflet we were able to quote numerous golden opinions of Thomas Harrison and his work. Harrison, C.R. Cockerell had written in 1823 " . . . has a spark divine." "The most classical and scientific architect of his day," Lord Elgin had observed in 1835. "Only his isolation in Chester and a natural diffidence prevented him from becoming a national figure like Soane or Smirke," Howard Colvin had written in his *Dictionary of British Architects*. Pevsner had described the Lyceum as " . . . one of the finest early buildings in Liverpool". Yet of the six buildings Harrison had worked on in the city all except the Lyceum had been demolished or altered out of recognition.

Though the Lyceum was now simply a club, its origins were of great interest. In the 1750s a small group of Liverpool gentlemen began to meet regularly to discuss literary subjects and to read periodicals and books. On 1 May 1758 they founded the Liverpool Library, the first subscription library in England. As the library grew it moved more than once to new premises and at their annual meeting on 13 May 1800 the proprietors agreed to raise funds for a new building combining library, news room and coffee room. Three hundred subscribers at twelve guineas were sought, but so numerous were the applicants that it was agreed to extend the membership to eight hundred. Thomas Harrison's design had been chosen in preference to that of John Foster, the Corporation's able Surveyor, principally on grounds of cost, and the building was completed and opened on 1 July 1802 at the cost of £11,399.

ABOVE: The newsroom at the Lyceum. Dating from 1802–03 its Grecian *gravitas* anticipates the interiors of London Clubs by 20 years.

Internally the main features were a very handsome circular domed library, which continued in being until 1942 when the books were sold off to a circulating library, and the News Room which, in the grandeur of its proportions, its chaste Grecian decoration and its *gravitas*, anticipated the Pall Mall club interiors of the 1820s. The Club history recorded that, as many of those using the news room were shipowners importing cotton and other raw materials, a weather vane, linked to a dial set in the wall, was incorporated in the news room. From comfortable armchairs, they could observe when a favourable wind allowed ships waiting at the bar to proceed up the Mersey. The Lyceum had flourished all through the nineteenth century and in 1903–4 a dining room and billiard room had been added on the roof. Two world wars, the Depression of the 1930s and Liverpool's declining fortunes after 1945 had reduced the number of members and thoughts of selling the site for redevelopment had been prompted by approaches by property companies.

The villain of the piece in the first instance seemed to be British Rail. In 1959 the Club had learnt that the British Railways Board was considering the redevelopment of the adjoining Central Station site and both parties decided it might be advantageous to offer the sites jointly. Matters progressed slowly but in 1966 Central Station closed and five years later consent was granted for the demolition of the Lyceum on the basis that the site was essential to the development of the new Liverpool Loop railway. The proprietors of the Lyceum agreed to sell the Club to Town and City Properties as part of a joint development but in the event Town and City could not reach agreement with British Rail and withdrew. British Rail then went ahead and built a smaller station leaving the Lyceum standing. The City Planning Office then drew up a brief for the site, acknowledging that consent had been granted to the Lyceum but stressed the strong public feeling against demolition and added, "Developers are requested to retain it if possible by rehabilitating it. Similarly consideration should be given to the retention of No. 7, Bold Street, the old Palatinate Club." The Palatinate Club was indeed a handsome building but it had been empty and early in 1978 had been demolished by British Rail – in what looked to us like a pre-emptive strike.

British Rail had invited tenders on the basis of this brief but only two had been received, from French Kier Property Investments and Kingsforth Property Holdings. The French Kier plans, dated 1977, followed the City brief and left the Lyceum out of the development, and suggested an L-shaped shopping arcade behind it, with entrances in Waterloo Place and Bold Street so that it formed a new covered pedestrian way. The Kingsforth Property Holdings scheme required the demolition of the Lyceum and it was this scheme British Rail had chosen.

By the middle of June, Peter Shore, the Secretary of State for the Environment, had received such a barrage of protest from people in Liverpool that he had apparently begun to think the unthinkable – to revoke the listed building consent and compensate the club. British Rail called a meeting of all the principal national bodies to review the situation. I was abroad at the time, as it happened fortunately, for one of the civil servants quoted in confidence Mr Shore's latest thinking and this was leaked after the meeting to the press, at which British Rail threatened to withdraw from all negotiations. If I had been there I would undoubtedly have been blamed.

Instead I found myself driving north to Derby on a Saturday morning in July for a special presentation of the Kingsforth proposals. During the hour long presentation every argument pointed in one direction: the Lyceum had to be demolished if any development was to take place, otherwise the site would be sterilized for ever. This was positively the last chance for a redevelopment, providing jobs and helping retain Liverpool's position as a major regional shopping centre. If we, the conservationists, opposed the scheme a key site in the heart of the city would go to waste and shoppers would go elsewhere. It was powerful stuff, and it ended with a flourish. The developer would dismantle the facade of the Lyceum stone by stone at his own expense and contribute £5,000 towards its re-erection below the Anglican Cathedral. Now was the time for us all to work together and to help raise the remaining £25,000 needed to cover the cost of moving it.

The idea of the facade surviving simply as a folly, and no doubt covered with every graffito imaginable within a month, was wholly unacceptable, and curiously the artist's impression showed the rebuilt front standing on a slope running in exactly the opposite direction to the slant at which it stood. So the carefully numbered stones would have to be rejigged, hardly satisfactory in a neo-classical building where every stone – and they were large stones – had been cut to the measurements of the architect. My companion, Randolph Langenbach, then spoke eloquently on the latest experience of shopping centres in America, that it was much better to have the principal, or anchor, store inside a shopping centre rather than on a corner, as Kingsforth proposed, as this would mean all the other shops would be on the route to the main store, and gain custom as a result, and hence be easier to let. If the anchor store was in the most prominent and accessible position everything else would be a backwater. Thus the point of total disagreement was reached and in a typically English way the developer took us off to an excellent lunch in his home nearby.

About a month later on 3 August came glorious news. Peter Shore was revoking the listed building consent to demolish. But on reading the press release it transpired he was simply "considering" whether he should do this and inviting the City Corporation's views. More important, he had for the time being prohibited the Council from granting planning permission on the site. Now the second blight on the future of the Lyceum became clear. The reason why only two developers had come forward in the first place was that the City Council was insisting that the developer provided, free and gratis, an overhead road across Ranelagh Street to provide access for delivery lorries to the block on the other side of the street, which in due course the Corporation was to develop. One section of this road actually existed, built by British Rail over the new station and looking like some giant piece of modern sculpture stranded on an empty building site. This road presupposed the whole block across the street would be demolished, which again was a wretched proposition as it was a lively mix of different frontages containing a great many small shops. Under pressure, the City Corporation eventually agreed to drop the overhead road requirement opening the way to finding a developer for British Rail's site behind the Lyceum. Eventually came the news we had been waiting for: Peter Shore, in response to overwhelming public concern, had decided to revoke the listed building consent and acquire the building from the Club.

This left the future use of the building uncertain so, with Ken Martin, Chairman of the Merseyside Civic Society, we drew up a scheme for the use of the building. The essence of this was that the City Registry Office was badly housed and wanted new premises. What better place for a wedding than the Lyceum? Would happy couples not be delighted to be photographed on the steps below the portico? With this we suggested a tourist information centre coupled with the new central station behind. The plans worked out neatly and provided the public the access we felt was essential after so much public campaigning.

Following the general election in April 1979 came a bombshell. Michael Heseltine, the new Secretary of State, had been to Liverpool and thrown the future of the building once again into question. "My predecessor," he said "as an act of faith decided to purchase the Club with the underlying implication that the State would then spend between £¾ and £1½ million on restoration works. At that point we would have an empty but beautiful early nineteenth-century building

. . . we would not have a development that would create jobs, or stimulate economic activity, or make valuable use of an empty site." We did not know then that Michael Heseltine was to prove a champion of conservation and it seemed all was lost. Yet our argument still held. The shopping development could take place behind the Lyceum – and a use could be found for the building. A month later Mr Heseltine announced his decision. "The Lyceum will be purchased with public funds so that it can be rapidly restored." A new use would be found, either for public or commercial purposes. This was glorious news, and there we felt we should let matters rest for a while. Our proposals could be dusted down if need be. But first months, then years, went by and nothing happened. We nonetheless thought it wise to refrain from inquiring until June 1983 – fortuitously just the right moment as a reply came saying the Department of the Environment was negotiating with a potential purchaser, who was planning to clean the building and restore the principal interiors.

However, things went one better. An even stronger interest was suddenly expressed by the Post Office and on 27 March 1984, Patrick Jenkin, the Secretary of State, announced he had sold the Lyceum to the Post Office for £320,000. The contract stipulated the principal architectural features of the building should be preserved and restored. The Post Office scheme included a branch post office and philatelic retail centre – both the rotunda and the reading room would survive substantially unaltered, while later additions above the parapet would be removed. Even the economics were more favoured than had been anticipated. It had been said it would cost at least half a million to revoke the listed building consent; in the event Michael Heseltine spent £575,000 in 1980 on buying the building, a further £60,000 on essential repairs, and almost exactly half was recouped by the sale to the Post Office. The cost was well below the £¾–1½ million Michael Heseltine had feared in 1979.

"You've picked a real loser this time," I remember being told in 1978 on my return from Moscow by a close and sanguine colleague at the outset of the campaign to save the Lyceum. It only goes to show that however late the hour, however overwhelming the odds, no fine historic building is a lost cause until it is physically demolished.

JUBILEE HALL

When I first went to work at *Country Life* in April 1968 the magazine still occupied the handsome offices commissioned by its founder and proprietor Edward Hudson from Sir Edwin Lutyens in 1904. The street facade was a deliberate play on Wren's courtyard at Hampton Court. I moved into an office with John Cornforth on the *piano nobile* lit by an enormous tall sash window – with the characteristic thick glazing bars of early sash windows. From here there was a splendid view over the Covent Garden market – then still very much a going concern – but immediately in the foreground, indeed hardly more than twenty or thirty feet from our window was another Edwardian building, the Jubilee Hall or foreign flower market, built the same year as the *Country Life* building to the designs of the now forgotten practice of Lander, Bedells and Crompton.

The Jubilee Hall was another essay in "Wrenaissance" but without the finesse of Lutyens or the superb brickwork and masonry, but distinctly a product of the surge of interest in English baroque at the turn of the century. The architectural features were concentrated at the corners, which were treated like pavilions with vertical bands of quoins and a broken pediment on both floors.

I mention this because one morning, as I was sitting in the *Country Life* office, a scaffold was erected and workmen set to on one of the pediments of the west end of the Jubilee Hall with high pressure drills and blasted away. It was a lengthy task but eventually every projecting moulding had been removed and they began work on the matching pediment on the north west corner. The purpose, I discovered a few days later, was to enable a lightweight shed to be built right up against the building, creating a covered area which was to be known as the Jubilee Market. It was a barbarous piece of mutilation and I remember reflecting long and carefully – did it really matter? My eventual conclusion was simple: what a waste. Here was a sound building, very much part of the market scene, which could well have been extended without damage if only someone had given it a moment's thought or if the building had been protected in some way. Little did I know then that ten years later I was to become embroiled in a fierce and hard-fought campaign to achieve just this – a campaign which like so many others looked completely outgunned but which succeeded with startling suddenness, when evidence emerged of political meddling in Whitehall.

All this was some ten years later. The editorial department of *Country Life* was now enjoying a lofty prospect from the twenty-second floor of Colonel Seifert's soaring King's Reach Tower, just to the south of Blackfriars Bridge and the first floor of the Jubilee Hall had become a highly successful Sports Hall. The restoration of the central market buildings in Covent Garden was now nearing completion and the whole area had taken on new life. Just one remnant survived of the original GLC proposal to flatten the whole neighbourhood and build a six lane road parallel with the Strand through the middle: this was the plan to redevelop the site of the Jubilee Hall. The Conservative GLC, backed by the planning team in Covent Garden, had clung to this with unflinching tenacity.

The argument put forward was that the demolition of the Jubilee Hall offered an opportunity to recreate something of the feeling of Inigo Jones's original piazza. This view was put, not without sarcasm, by Mr. William Bell, Chairman of the GLC's Historic Buildings Committee, at a Council meeting on 2 October 1979. "I can only repeat it is difficult to attribute any historic interest to a building constructed as late as 1904 by virtually unknown architects which, following its total failure as a market, spent the last half century as a potato warehouse . . . Throughout the decision process on Covent Garden it was consistently agreed by all parties that the re-creation of the formality of the Covent Garden Market square was of vital importance and represented an unrepeatable opportunity to give London a new square of great historic significance and architectural distinction . . . The retention of the existing undistinguished hall would render this aim impossible and perpetuate the present most unsatisfactory visual enclosure on the south side." I could never agree with this point of view. All Inigo Jones's buildings around the piazza, except the church, had gone. The character of Covent Garden, not only to Londoners but (thanks to the film *My Fair Lady*) to people all over the world, lay in its great collection of market buildings. Having witnessed the tragic destruction of Les Halles, the great iron and glass market in Paris, and the large hole left on that site for many years, I was convinced of the need to preserve and find new uses for the whole collection of market buildings in Covent Garden.

With the Jubilee Hall use was not a problem – the Sports Hall was flourishing and very keen to renew the original five year lease. It was also an excellent example of practical low cost conversion – all the work of installation costing just £70,000. The hall was in constant demand for a wide range of sports – netball, volley ball, football, basketball, badminton, roller skating, aikido, trampolining and keep fit. But the GLC remained completely intransigent and adduced every possible argument to belittle the building and its use. A curiously worded brief was circulated round County Hall saying, "It is understood that many local children no longer use the centre having become alienated by its new image and other clientele." We reacted vigorously and circulated all GLC members with the riposte that the hall was used by a wide range of "local youth clubs – the Basement Youth Club, Shelton Street, the Soho Youth Club, the 3 C's Youth Club and the Gainsford Club, three local nurseries and two primary schools". The Jubilee Hall was running its own incisive campaign, with two brilliant posters designed and produced *gratis* by a local advertising agency and a whole series of events and demonstrations including group jogs to County Hall.

The GLC based its case on the fact that it had bought the site at development value: the £1.35 million outlay, they claimed, including interest charges, could only be recouped if the building was demolished. The Jubilee Hall team produced an alternative conservation scheme to show this was not the case. By building on the site adjoining the hall it was possible to create approximately as much floor space as would have been allowed in a new building.

The Jubilee Hall stood in a conservation area so permission would have to be obtained before it was demolished. If the GLC sought the consent, it would be decided by the Secretary of State, and this would almost certainly mean a public inquiry where we could put the case for preservation. However we were convinced the GLC would sidestep this by asking a developer to make the application, in which case the GLC itself could grant the consent forthwith. So at the same time we mounted pressure to get the Jubilee Hall listed – principally on the grounds of group value, that it

was part of a collection of buildings that gave Covent Garden its essential character. There is no doubt in my mind that architecturally it formed a very important counterpoint to the elegant Regency arcades on the south side of the central market buildings. Viewed from the top of Southampton Street with the Flower Market (now the London Transport Museum) in the background, it summed up what Covent Garden was all about. This was not the classical symmetry of Inigo Jones's long lost piazza and arcades, but that of market buildings which, although of different dates and styles, were complementary in colour and building materials.

However, Ministers were adamant in refusing all requests for listing. On 18 January 1980 Hector Munro, Under Secretary of State at the Department of the Environment wrote saying: "We have thoroughly considered the merits of the building and, like our predecessors in office, have concluded it would not be right to add it to the statutory list." The Jubilee Hall looked increasingly doomed until suddenly Ian MacNicol received a copy of a long letter from one of Hector Munro's predecessors in the Labour government, Reg Freeson, to Michael Heseltine, dated 12 June 1980. This contained a nugget of information that transformed the position. In December 1977 Ministers had received a minute which, Mr. Freeson wrote, explained that "Jubilee Hall was not recommended for listing in 1972, but at the time DOE inspectors were unable to carry out a full inspection. The survey investigator – a Mr Green, I think – had now been able to examine the building thoroughly, inside and out, and reported that it was altogether more interesting than could be expected at first sight. He judged the building to be of Grade II quality and recommended its inclusion in the statutory list." This was presumably Michael Green, the unsung hero of Covent Garden who had drawn up the original list of 200 buildings with which Geoffrey Rippon as Secretary of State had killed the GLC's massive redevelopment plans at one single blow. From our point of view the recommendation to list was vital because the Secretary of State for the Environment has a duty to list buildings of architectural or historic interest. He cannot simply refuse to list buildings because of

PREVIOUS PAGE: The Piazza at Covent Garden with the Jubilee Hall on the right. It was only saved from demolition after an intense public campaign.

other considerations such as the potential redevelopment value of the site or the views of fellow politicians in County Hall. However, he does take such points into account when determining an ensuing application to demolish.

Mr. Freeson went on to explain that Lady Birk had decided to proceed with listing but the Department had then received a long and powerful letter from the Covent Garden Team headed by Mr G.R. Holland, setting out the GLC's view of the financial implications of listing and concluding, in Mr. Freeson's words, "that GLC studies had clearly shown that conversion of the Hall for an economic use was impracticable, so there would be a very heavy loss of public funds." Following this listing did not proceed. Mr. Freeson went on to say that statements made in the House of Lords by Lord Mowbray and Lord Stourton, and by Mr. Munro in the House of Commons to the effect that both the present Secretary of State and his predecessor had decided the Jubilee Hall was not of sufficient interest to qualify for listing were incorrect.

With Ian MacNicol we promptly took a copy of Mr. Freeson's letter to our solicitors, Gouldens, where David Cooper advised us to go for *Mandamus*, a court order to force the Minister to do what he is obliged to do under statute. A solicitor's letter went off to the Secretary of State enclosing Mr. Freeson's letter stating this was clear evidence that the building had been considered of statutory quality, and that we would issue a writ unless it was listed. Within twenty-four hours the reply came. Jubilee Hall was listed – on 3 July 1980. Officially it was stated the building had been listed on the advice of the Historic Buildings Council, but there was no doubt in our minds that it could never have happened so speedily but for the opportunity for action provided by Mr. Freeson's letter. The reaction from the conservatives at County Hall was outrage – expressed in furious terms in a debate that very night. But Willie Bell, our former adversary, proved a voice of moderation saying, "I am sure this council would be wise to accept that there is a weight of public opinion, nationally as well as locally, in favour of retaining the existing building and that we should agree to look at this whole matter again."

The GLC now drew up a new planning brief providing for the retention of the hall. During this consultation period the Jubilee Hall

team established that the first floor could continue as a Sports Hall. The team then combined with local groups and traders to form a Development Consortium and established that the GLC would sell the site to them if they could obtain finance. The figures, alas, just would not work. With the Sports Hall, and an element of public housing in the new building, there was just too much community rented space. At the last moment, however, the Consortium found a development company, Speyhawk, which was willing to do a joint scheme on similar lines. As I write the planning application has just gone in, and, if all goes smoothly, work on site will begin early in 1984. From SAVE's point of view the choice of Speyhawk is of special interest, as Speyhawk played a key role in the battle for Billingsgate Fish Market to which we now turn.

BILLINGSGATE

"Mr. Marcus Binney really cannot be allowed to have his cake and eat it," wrote the Chairman of the Billingsgate and Leadenhall Markets Committe in *The Times* on 23 April 1980. He was replying to a letter of my own published five days earlier championing the cause of the newly listed Billingsgate market. He continued, "For him to have cited Covent Garden in support of his case for retention of market buildings is astonishing. The tax payer has had to find £13 million to pay for that move, in part because the new market authority was unable to obtain the value of the old sites which had been listed. A parallel case, yes, but it proves the opposite to Mr Binney's claim." And there was more in the same vein. But it is my experience that in the middle of every campaign someone always weighs in saying the economics of conserving an old building are nonsense, and the only real test comes when the building is eventually sold or restored. The Chairman of the Market Committee was understandably concerned to recoup the £7.4 million cost of the move to new premises on the Isle of Dogs. In the end Billingsgate Fish Market and the adjoining lorry park were sold, on the basis of a

OPPOSITE: The river front at Billingsgate Fish Market. The City Corporation was set on demolition but these plans received a sudden setback when the market was spotlisted by Michael Heseltine in April 1980.

scheme preserving the existing building as we had advocated, for a staggering £22 million. But in April 1980 that was all in the future.

Michael Heseltine, Secretary of State for the Environment, had spotlisted Billingsgate Market on 2 April. The outcry in the City had been immediate and fierce. At a press conference held eight days later the joint committee of traders' and employees' representatives claimed the listing had put "the future employment of about 2000 who work there in jeopardy", so *The Times* reported the next day. On television I even heard it claimed that the future of the entire British fishing industry was under threat.

Most popular of all was the story that Billingsgate market would collapse when the cold store in the basement began to unfreeze. "What happens when London's giant iceberg melts," ran a headline in the London *Evening News* magazine on 28 March 1980, and this story must have been printed hundreds of times all over the world. The article, by Keith Blogg, continued: "Some 32,700 square feet of deep freeze, plus an estimated 20,000 square feet of permafrost, built up layer upon chilling layer over half a century, have now joined the venerable foundations in supporting the towering iron columns and soaring girdered nave of this great temple to the capital's fishing trade." And there was more in the same colourful vein. "When the iceberg melts, runs one theory, Billingsgate will topple like a house of cards. First the walls will crack, then the pillars will lean at a crazy angle and finally, the roof will crash 60 feet onto the concourse below." A cold store expert was quoted as saying brickwork deeply permeated by frost was like a strawberry which looked perfectly good after it had been frozen. "But the cells have been destroyed. Once the ice melts the thing turns to mush." The City Architect's office made much the same noises, talking of groundheave and consequential stress on vertical members. But as if the ice story was not good enough there was another hardly less colourful reason given in a little booklet entitled *The Corporation's Year 1979*: "Although the present Billingsgate Market is less than a hundred years old, the corrosive effects of fish juice mean it has to be rebuilt."

SAVE entered the lists for Billingsgate with such vigour because we were convinced that its preservation and reuse would work in economic terms; and if we could prove this in the City of

ABOVE: View from the Monument across Billingsgate to HMS Belfast and Tower Bridge. The lorry park on the right of the Fish Market was to prove its salvation – with planning permission for a new building on this site the complex was sold for £22 million and the market is to be restored.

London, where development values were so high, it would be a powerful argument in fighting for buildings in city centres all over the country. Architecturally, the glory of Billingsgate was its riverside site. Between the Houses of Parliament and the Tower of London there are very few buildings of character or distinction right on the waterfront. For much of the way they are set back behind the Embankment. Then, in the City itself, in place of the great cliff of warehouses that once rose sheer from the river, there was a long parade of boxlike offices interspersed with multistorey car parks. Billingsgate with its pavilions, mansard roofs, dormers and gilded dolphins had once struck an immensely festive note on the waterfront, and could do once again if only the wretched row of sheds built out on a jetty on the river edge were removed. From the river terrace there is the most spectacular view of the Thames in London with Tower Bridge seen in all its majesty in full silhouette, and

HMS Belfast moored resplendently on the far bank.

Inside, Billingsgate consisted of two parallel market halls divided by a double line of Doric columns but the boldness of the original design had been greatly marred by the introduction of portakabin type offices down the centre and along the southern side. These, however, could easily be removed, restoring the halls to their original proportions and opening up the view from one hall to the other. All the traders' names over the stalls were painted in a splendid livery of green and gold, which, with the deep red of the cast iron columns, provided an excellent colour scheme for a restored market. Also of interest were the glass roofs over the market halls. Sir Horace Jones, the architect, had written, "The roof of a market must, or rather, ought to be light, airy and cool in summer, and whilst admitting light and air, it must keep out wet and cold in the winter." At Billingsgate he provided for this by the use of moving glass louvres. But at the ends of the halls, where the roofs met the north and south ranges, Jones introduced a virtuoso display of carpentry with free-standing ribs branching and interlocking like the remarkable vaults found in central European churches at the very end of the middle ages.

Sir Horace Jones, the architect of Billingsgate, was a characteristic example of Victorian success, rising by diligence and application to become President of the Royal Institute of British Architects in 1881 and earning a knighthood in 1886. He was responsible for many of London's best known Victorian landmarks – Tower Bridge, which he designed with the engineer J. Wolfe Barry, Smithfield Market and Leadenhall Market. Architecturally Smithfield is more impressive than Billingsgate and Leadenhall more unusual and charming. But Billingsgate had the most spectacular and visible site and the greatest potential for improvement.

Even before the good news of Michael Heseltine's listing on 2 April 1980 we had begun work on a scheme to show how the market could be preserved on competitive terms. In October the year before, I had been to San Francisco and spent some time looking at converted buildings on the waterfront. When San

OPPOSITE ABOVE: The elaborate flying ribs of Billingsgate's timber roof. Even after the building had been saved it was uncertain whether these would be retained.
BELOW: The Fishmongers' Stalls at Billingsgate.

Francisco is mentioned most people immediately think of Fisherman's Wharf, but Fisherman's Wharf is essentially a collection of quite small modern buildings in vernacular style, mainly restaurants and shops. In terms of preservation and reuse the really spectacular conversion is the shopping centre created in the former Ghirardelli chocolate factory dating from 1893–1916, and now known as Ghirardelli Square. By a lucky chance when I was there in October 1979 an exhibition had been mounted explaining the history and economics of the project. William M. Roth had purchased the factory in 1962, "determined to show that his native city could change without destroying the best from its past and that it was a sound investment to adapt historic architecture to new job-creating uses." The complex was still flourishing fifteen years after it had opened, so its success was not simply due to novelty: indeed it had become one of San Franciso's top dozen tourist attractions. In all there were 75 retail shops, 16 eating places and a theatre. Very few of the stores or restaurants were part of chains and there had been remarkably few tenant changes since 1964. In 1979 the Square was providing employment for 800 people, generating £1 million in salaries, while minimum business hours (10 am to 9 pm during the summer and from Thanksgiving to Christmas) ensured the complex was alive for most of the day.

The year before I had been to Quincy Market in Boston, where the old market buildings had been converted into a flourishing complex of shops and stalls, selling food and wares of every kind. During a visit to the developer's office I learnt that the Quincy Market had the highest turnover of any shopping centre in the United States, more than one and a half times its nearest competitor. "We had to be tough on the buildings," they explained, and certainly the alterations had been quite drastic. For example, all the original windows had been removed and plate glass inserted. I wondered if this was necessary and whether more of the original character could not be retained in a future conversion without damaging the financial potential.

The thought in my mind was how to transfer the American experience to Billingsgate. By good fortune, shortly after my return I happened to meet Hugh Cantlie, a chartered surveyor who had made a study of shopping centres while working for MEPC, the

144

property company, and had recently been directing the construction of an office block in Munich. He had experience in exactly the two areas we needed and could work on the economics of a shopping centre in the old market and provide a valuation of a new office block on the adjoining lorry park. But to do a scheme we needed an architect. Over Christmas 1979 I had a sharp clash over the proposed new insurance market building at Lloyd's, where Richard Rogers, fresh from the laurels he had won for his Pompidou Centre in Paris, had been commissioned to replace Sir Edwin Cooper's Lloyd's Building of the 1920s. I felt that the quality of Cooper's building had been badly underestimated and leapt to its defence.

This is a saga which deserves recounting at another time and place but it was clear that very few people were willing to make a stand over a 1920s building. The Committee of the Society for the Protection of Ancient Buildings, for example, were given a lunchtime tour of the old building and shown the Rogers proposals and came away, I was told, quite enamoured of them. SAVE cast a fly over Richard Rogers to see if he was interested in cooperating on a scheme for Billingsgate. He responded favourably, and it was a lucky choice, for very soon after the City Corporation enthusiastically approved his Lloyd's design and this meant they had to take the Billingsgate scheme seriously – for all their violent opposition to the listing.

The actual work on the drawings was done by two of Richard Rogers' colleagues, Alan Stanton and Ian Ritchie, who had set up independently as Chrysalis Architects but still worked very closely with his office. The proposals we evolved restored the market building as far as possible to its original appearance, with shops and stalls in the western hall and eating in the eastern hall, the idea was to adapt the Quincy Market layout and have long trestle tables and a series of different food shops. People would then buy food from different stalls – a seafood stall, a charcoal grill, a cake stall, an ice cream counter. It would in fact be a pub lunch on a grand scale, with a floor area more like a Munich beer hall. In addition, we proposed there would be a first floor restaurant on the waterfront, and we suggested the two previous taverns in the end pavilions should be re-established.

Billingsgate also has spectacular vaulted cellars and we planned to open these up by means of escalators, with a mezzanine level of shops and a further area for drinking and eating below. Initial reaction from the City planning officers and from councillors was sceptical. "It may work at Covent Garden but here in the City, Billingsgate is on a limb and it will be quite dead in the evening." But we perservered and later found very strong interest from the City Retailers Association, who provided us with an amazing statistic: one shop had closed every two and a half weeks in the City over the last ten years. Not surprisingly they were very strongly in support of a substantial increase in shopping such as we proposed.

And the shopping it transpired worked in financial terms. The City in its planning brief (which they refused to issue formally to us) specified a plot ratio of no more than five to one across the whole site – of which at least two fifths was to be shopping or retailing. Hugh Cantlie worked out that all this shopping could be accommodated in the old market buildings, and that the maximum office space permitted could be incorporated in a new building on the lorry park, which would just conform, if only just, to the likely height restrictions – set by existing buildings to the east. Hugh Cantlie made endless calculations on rentals comparing our scheme with an entirely new building and concluded eventually that our scheme provided at worst a shortfall of 8 per cent, and indeed might well level peg with an entirely new development.

The third complicating factor was the archaeological potential of the lorry park, which the archaeologists considered to be the most important single remaining site in London. They were very concerned that the preservation of the old market might reduce or even remove any possibility of a major excavation. Chrysalis Architects therefore went to great lengths to show how provision for archaeology could be made if necessary, even after a new building had begun, and in the event the whole development timetable allowed more than six months for an extensive dig.

The SAVE proposals were published in July 1980 and met, on the whole, with a very good response. The City Corporation's application for consent to demolish the old market building remained, though in suspense: then on 20 November at the Court of Common Council the City voted itself what is called a deemed planning consent for a development almost exactly on the lines we had proposed. Following this the City Surveyor and St Quintin, the estate agents, produced an offer document inviting tenders on the basis of this permission by noon on 28 August 1981. The date worried us considerably. Was not this just the time when all successful property developers would be on their yachts in the Mediterranean? Wishing to pursue our scheme as far as we could, we approached Trevor Osborne, the chairman of Speyhawk, who I had met while we were both serving as members of Lord Montagu's Committee on alternative uses for historic buildings. The City was simply asking for bids, and a description of proposals – no architects drawings were required. Trevor Osborne and Hugh Cantlie had long discussions as to what bid to make and eventually decided on a figure of £19.6 million. This went off by messenger to arrive a few minute before noon on the appointed day. No self-respecting property developer, I learnt, would dream of making a bid until the very, very last moment. What happens if the messenger gets stuck in a traffic jam to this day I do not know.

Soon after we learnt that Speyhawk was among a number of bids accepted for further examination – four in all, we later discovered. The City Corporation now added a new dimension: could our scheme be adapted to provide premises for the London Commodity Exchange. One of the schemes, we knew, was already providing a commodity exchange in the old building, but we considered the market halls were too high and too large for this purpose. Trevor Osborne was nonetheless able to show that the Commodity Market could be accommodated in the new building. Hugh Cantlie and I had carried out a fair amount of discussions with members of the various markets which might make up the proposed commodity exchange and been left in great doubt as to whether many of them would anyway be willing to make the move to new premises. As it happened the Commodity Exchange eventually withdrew.

The day came when the Corporation announced the winning tender – S. & W. Berisford, though as we understood the SAVE-Speyhawk scheme had been the runner up. But this was still a victory. The old market building was to be saved and reused, following a scheme very much on the lines we suggested. The only problem was that in choosing the highest bidder, without agreeing the details of the scheme, the Corporation had left the way open for more radical alterations to the market buildings than might be consistent with preserving its character. But the Corporation did not really care and neither, it transpired at a public inquiry, did the Greater London Council. The main point at issue, it became clear at the inquiry, was Berisford's plans to shorten the market halls by one bay at either end. This meant a reduction from six bays to four bays, and since the end bays had the most interesting roofs this was to mean the loss of the best part of the interior. But neither the City nor the GLC objected and Michael Heseltine accepted his inspector's recommendation and ruled in the developer's favour. But the character of the market halls, the architects insist, will be jealously safeguarded. We await opening day with the keenest interest.

CINEMAS

"No doubt soon Mr. Binney and his supporters of SAVE will turn their enthusiasm to the super cinemas of the 1930s, and the community will be expected to maintain these vast edifices with occasional conducted tours." So ran a letter to *The Sunday Times* on 23 November 1975 from the Rev. Jack Webb expressing indignation at SAVE's support of local attempts to prevent the demolition of Holy Trinity Tunbridge Wells. My reply was never published for the excellent reason that two local people had written forceful replies defending their plans to turn Holy Trinity into an arts and drama centre – which has now been done with considerable success. Mr. Webb was right on one point – the outlook for the great Odeons and Gaumonts of the interwar years was indeed gloomy, and but for the advent of Bingo, few would have survived at all.

Six years later, quite unexpectedly, in Atlanta, Georgia, I came across a newly restored 'super' cinema which, in an instant, filled me with new optimism that cinemas could survive. I had gone with my wife to prepare an article for *Country Life* on a remarkable classical house of the 1920s by a brilliant architect Philip Shutze who all his life had designed in traditional styles. I had spent the afternoon looking at his buildings in downtown Atlanta with Mrs. Julian Carr, and just as we were driving out she mentioned we were approaching a cinema which her son had rescued from demolition and was now restoring. She stopped the car: I had imagined quite a modest building, but the Atlanta Fox was vast, as large as a major opera house, and extremely handsome and colourful. The style was Moorish and the two street elevations were faced in alternating bands of buff and cream brick, in emulation of mosques in Cairo. While many cinemas in Britain consist of a show facade and huge bare flanks, the Fox was architecture in the round, with a side elevation as elaborate and beautifully finished as the main front.

The Fox I discovered had been conceived originally not just as a cinema but as a masonic hall – the Yaarab Temple of the Ancient Arabic Order of the Nobles of the Mystic Shrine. The Shriners, as they are called, are one of a series of Masonic groups with exotic or oriental rites – others are the Tall Cedars of Lebanon and the Veiled Prophets of the Enchanted Realm. It sounds pure Hollywood and it was, inside as well as out. The Atlanta Temple was conceived as early as 1916 but it was not till early in 1928 that the plans were formally announced in local newspapers. Soon after construction began spiralling costs forced the Shriners to enter partnership with William K. Fox. However, they reserved the right to use their 5000 seater auditorium at least six times a year.

The architects were an Atlanta firm, Marye, Alger and Vinour. Mayre was quoted as saying boldly, "Although the building is in no way a copy of any one oriental structure, it tries to embody the entire scope of Mahommedan art." Oliver J. Vinour, the principal designer, was French. He had studied at the École des Beaux Arts. A contemporary newspaper clip suggests he had turned to two sources, picture books on Nubia and the Holy Land, and a stack of picture postcards a friend had brought back from a grand tour of the Middle East. But the Fox is far from a collage of borrowings, rather a brilliant piece of planning and visual drama, consistently lively and varied in the detail.

The main entrance to the cinema is at the end of a deep arcade which has a stencilled ceiling in green, red and gold, and silver honeycomb niches along the walls. When I arrived the final touches of paintwork and silvering were being applied. Some of the great cinemas of the 1920s open into a foyer of stupendous dimensions but here Marye and Vinour created an atmosphere of mystery appropriate to a Mahommedan palace. As you ascend from level to level what lies beyond is unpredictable. The mezzanine promenade is suggestive of an Ottoman seraglio with screens of columns enclosing divans where patrons could sit in the intervals. The dress circle above presents a dramatic perspective of flattened horseshoe arches. The ladies' and gentlemen's retiring rooms are palatial, and though they did not glory in names such as the Harem Parlour and the Caliph's Den (like those at the Avalon Cinema in Chicago) they are no less exotic. In the ladies', Tutankahmun takes over from Mahommedan, reflecting Howard Carter's discoveries in 1922. The ladies' lounge foyer has a towering beehive ceiling and a chimney framed by Egyptian columns with papyrus capitals. The chairs are modelled on Tutankahmun's throne.

The climax is naturally the auditorium. There were two schools of design for cinema amphitheatres in the 1920s – the "hard-top" and the "atmospheric". The hard-top followed the Victorian and Edwardian tradition of domes and luscious gilded plasterwork: the atmospheric sought to create the illusion of an outdoor courtyard under a moonlit sky, with stage set architecture around the walls. Ceilings were painted a noctural blue, with bulbs set in the patterns of the major constellations of stars. The creator of the atmospheric was John Eberson, and here Marye, Alger and Vinour had taken over his device of transforming the proscenium arch into a great bridge. The walls were designed in imitation of a fortified Islamic town, complete with gatehouses neatly containing the emergency exits. At the back huge striped tent tops, like canopies of state for some oriental potentate, spread out over the dress circle – these were not just decorative but ingeniously disguised sound baffles.

The Fox had opened on Christmas Day in 1929. In June 1932 both the Fox Corporation and the Yaarab Temple Building Company went bankrupt. Subsequent vicissitudes are worth recounting as an example of just how many reverses a fine building may have to endure before it finds a secure future. Two months later

OPPOSITE ABOVE: The side entrance of Atlanta's Fox cinema soon after it had been cleaned and restored. BELOW: The Fox auditorium. An 'atmospheric' interior with the ceiling treated as a night-time sky.

it had reopened only to close its doors again that December. Soon after it was sold at auction for a mere $75,000 to a theatre holding company owned by officers of the Yaarab Temple. When this collapsed the city of Atlanta took possession for non-payment of taxes. In 1935 Paramount Pictures stepped in. The Fox struggled on for nearly four decades until television, and the loss of the annual visit of the Metropolitan Opera to the new Atlanta Civic Centre spelled doom. Increasingly it looked as if the Fox would suffer the inglorious fate of demolition for a parking lot for the Southern Bell Telephone Tower which was to rise just behind it. Yet a public hearing in July 1974, held in the cinema to debate its future, brought an audience of 2,500. A trust, Atlanta Landmarks, was formed to save the Fox and secured $11,000 in state funds for a feasibility study on its future. A leading firm of economics consultants was retained and produced a report showing how the Fox could pay its way not as a cinema but a live entertainment centre. The cost of acquiring and repairing the building still had to be met from public subscription. The mayor announced an eight month moratorium on demolition and Beauchamp Carr, working through a major estate agency had acquired the rest of the land on the block with loans from the five major Atlanta banks, and swopped this land with Southern Bell in June 1975 for the Fox. The entire debt of $2.4 million was cleared in 1978 and the Fox now has a flourishing programme. Yul Brynner in *The King and I* and Nureyev and the Boston Ballet are but two of a continuous pageant of major events.

I thought the Fox's triumph must be unique until two years later I was walking past Loew's Theatre in Richmond. I remembered this from a visit some years before as a huge, bare-walled building like an ice store. Suddenly it was clean: the zigzag patterns of brickwork stood out and rich tilework ornament glowed in brilliant technicolour. Loew's Theatre had been restored as the Virginia Center for the Performing Arts – once again with the emphasis on live events, and was now back in full use. In its last incarnation I learnt it had been "Kung Fooed" – modernized in the early 1970s in keeping with Loew's macho image and painted over in deadpan yellow, browns, greys and blacks. But Kung Foo had brought only a short lease of life and Loew's had closed finally in 1979. Once again a consulting firm had been brought in to evaluate the economic return from a performing arts centre and they had boldly predicted a $7.3 million 'shot in the arm' to the Richmond economy in the first year, or $1.2 for every $1 invested in the centre. Nearly $5 million has been spent on refurbishing and equipping the new centre, providing acoustics that are compared to Philadelphia's Academy of Music. But the most spectacular result is the revival of the original decor, which in fact had cost less than $200,000.

The result has been described as "Metro-Goldwyn Medici" but, in fact, the style was dominantly Spanish baroque or rather Chirrugesque – a riot of ornament painted in brilliant colour. Once again it was an atmospheric rather than a hard-top, but this time the architect was John Eberson himself, inventor of the atmospheric cinema. On the first opening night it was reported that live parrots perched in the artificial trees, and a starry sky was projected across the ceiling. In the restoration however the architects, Marcellus Wright Cox & Smith claimed to have outdone Eberson. As well as an azure ceiling with pinhole lights suggesting the stars, and clouds superimposed by projectors, modern lighting techniques have made possible a whole spectrum of blues, and any time of day from dawn to midnight is now available at the press of a button. Microscopic paint samples have provided the evidence of the original colours and the new paint has been applied with rags to recreate the original raised swirling patterns. Modern technology has come to the aid of restoration: the original carpets have been rewoven by computer.

CHURCHES

"WE'LL HAVE YOUR BLOOD Marcus Binney, we'll have your blood." It was the evening of Wednesday, 13 July 1977, the preview of the Victoria and Albert exhibition, *Change and Decay: The Future of Our Churches*. I had been confronted by two officials responsible for operating the Church of England's redundant churches procedure. Their anger was understandable. The exhibition text panels were blunt, and constituted a hard attack on the Church Commissioners and the Pastoral Measure of 1968 which established formal declarations of redundancy. The statistics were startling. In 1976 the Church Commissioners had approved the demolition of one church every nine days – thirty-nine in the course of the year. One text panel, accompanying a slide programme portraying the demise of redundant churches in Leeds, was headed "The Vandals Charter". "In cities like Birmingham, Liverpool and Manchester," we said, "once a church is closed or made redundant, it becomes an immediate target for vandalism and often an invitation to arson. Every pane of glass is systematically smashed, every surface covered with graffiti, every remaining furnishing mutilated. Indeed, the state of degradation and defilement to which some churches are now reduced exceeds even the iconoclasm of the Reformation or the Commonwealth. In these circumstances, the Church of England's Pastoral Measure of 1968, which places every redundant church in a waiting period of at least one year, during which it is left obviously empty and deserted, has often proved little less than a

OPPOSITE: Elgin Place church, Glasgow in 1976. A fine example of Greek Revival, designed by John Burnet in 1856. It was painted for a television pop concert after ecclesiastical use had ceased.

vandal's charter." In Leeds the Diocese had been so embarrassed by the vandalized condition of St Mary's Quarry Hill, a fine Waterloo Commissioners' church, that they had only let us in on the condition that we took no photographs.

Within a month of the opening of the exhibition came some very good news. The Government had decided to make good a promise, first made in 1973, to provide up to £1 million a year towards the repair of historic churches which until then, had not been eligible for Historic Buildings Council grants.

This sounds curious but there was a good reason. Buildings in ecclesiastical use were exempt from the normal listed building and ancient monument controls, and successive Governments had taken the view, "no control, no money". For many years the Church of England had felt independence was its first priority.

Since 1977, Historic Buildings Council grants have transformed the outlook for historic churches all over the country. No less important is that the proportion of redundant churches being demolished has fallen while the figures for alternative use have risen impressively. There still remain many difficult cases where a solution is only achieved after a long hard battle. Experience has taught me that with effort and persistence, an acceptable solution can be found to the problem of almost all redundant churches, even where the church authorities have decided on demolition as the only way forward. A disused church is usually a sad, even agonizing sight, and may seem a reproach to those who have battled to keep it going only to abandon the struggle due to factors beyond their control. By this same token, a redundant church that takes on a new lease of life is all the more inspiring.

ST JOHN'S, READING

On a Saturday afternoon early in December 1981 I drove down to Reading with Matthew Saunders to attend a special mass celebrating the re-opening of the redundant church of St John as a Roman

OPPOSITE: St John's, Reading. A major campaign fiercely waged nationally and locally persuaded the Diocese and the Church Commissioners to abandon plans to demolish the church and instead sell it to the local Polish Roman Catholic community.

Catholic church for Reading's large Polish community. The church was packed. A Polish cardinal had come from Rome; war veterans stood in uniform before the altar steps and a brass band played from the gallery at the back of the church. This was indeed a glorious moment, not only for the Poles and for all their supporters and well-wishers, but for SAVE, as there was no church we had fought longer or harder to preserve, and no church where the Church Commissioners had proved so unyielding in their determination to proceed with demolition.

You see the broad spire of St John's as the train draws into Reading but its significance is principally as a very handsome local landmark dominating an attractive residential area of simple two-storey brick terraces. It was built in 1872–74 to the designs of W. A. Dixon in what Canon Basil Clarke, who had seen more parish churches than anyone else in England, described as "coarse and muscular thirteenth century French gothic". The masonry was unusually good with uneven courses of rugged stonework contrasting with crisp ashlar mouldings. And the detail was bold and lively – a charmingly diminutive arcade on the tower framing the windows of the ringing chamber and pairs of tall arched windows to the bell chamber above. The spire was all in smooth stone with slender lucarnes – the ecclesiastical equivalent of a dormer window – rising from the base. With the adjoining church school, also built to Dixon's designs, the whole composition made a very satisfying group, neatly encircled by a contemporary church wall, which eventually was to assume great and unexpected significance.

The scheme to demolish St John's had been approved by the Privy Council in December 1973, and as a result of this the Church Commissioners needed no further consent to demolish it. This was despite the fact that the church had shortly afterwards been listed by the Department of the Environment.

The reason why it had continued in use until the middle of 1978 was this: two parishes were uniting and both churches were to be demolished and sold to provide funds for a new multipurpose church centre a short distance away in Orts Road. The other church, St Stephen's, had been demolished but St John's was retained for use by both parishes until the new Church was ready. As it happened, St Stephen's was also a building of considerable interest: its architect

William White was very accomplished and a leading light in the Ecclesiological Society, carrying out much church building and restoration in Cornwall. He was also incidentally a great nephew of the famous naturalist Gilbert White of Selborne.

We were so concerned about the proposed demolition of St John's because since the scheme had been approved by the Privy Council, the Polish Roman Catholics had come forward and offered to buy the church for £15,000. They were then worshipping in another Anglican church but had to fit their services around those of the parish, and this meant their principal service on a Sunday had to be at midday which caused understandable problems, not least in cooking Sunday lunch. Nonetheless they had an average congregation of 300 every Sunday: with their own church they felt they could double this figure. St John's was in good condition and this seemed an ideal solution. With so many redundant churches, the problem is finding a suitable alternative use. Here there was the best possible solution so we decided to make it a test case. And there was a second string in case the Poles withdrew: a scheme to convert the church to residential use for which Reading Council had approved £250,000. This would mean the loss of the interior but allow the church and tower to survive as a landmark.

We sought maximum publicity. We held a press conference in Prince Henry's Room above Fleet Street, at which a rather amusing incident occurred, fortunately not the setback it might have been. We had asked one of St John's supporters from Reading to come, and amidst all the complexities of the Church Commissioners procedures one journalist seized on a remark he had made. "Excuse me, did you say this is the second most important Victorian church in Britain?" "No," came the answer. "I said it was the second most important Victorian church in Reading."

Meanwhile the Bishop of Reading had spoken out locally under the heading of an article: *I was not ordained to become a museum curator.* "They don't want to be looking over their shoulders at the old church," he said. "It is all to do with Christian ideas of death and resurrection." A statement issued to the paper on 13 September 1978 amplified this. The agreement to build the new church had been based on the fact that both St Stephen's and St John's would be demolished. "To go back now on this one aspect would betray not only the congregation of St John's but also the congregation of St Stephen's who have already sacrificed their much loved building for the sake of the vision which is now taking substance . . . the death must be a real death in order for the resurrection in Orts Road also to be a reality.''

The Church Commissioners continued to resist all appeals and on 29 September I had a letter from Mr William Harris, chairman of their Redundant Churches Committee, saying that the Commissioners had reviewed the case carefully and decided demolition should proceed as soon as possible. "I must make it clear that their decision is final," he concluded.

Then came the news that Pope Paul had been elected. Rashly we sent a telegram of congratulation inviting his support for the campaign to save St John's for his compatriots. This rebounded on us as the next I heard was a telephone call from one of the leaders of the Polish community in Reading saying they were very unhappy lest this was taken to suggest they felt they had some special claim on his attention amidst all his other cares. Every avenue had been explored with no success and he felt they should say no more. Suddenly it looked hopeless.

There was, in fact, one more hurdle for the Church Commissioners to surmount – the church wall, barely three feet high. Reading District Council had taken the view that listed building consent was required to demolish the wall, and the adjoining church hall. The Commissioners needed to take the wall down to bring demolition tackle in. So they applied for consent to dismantle and recreate the wall with the greatest care. The Reading planning committee resolutely refused. Stalemate ensued, and then suddenly the Commissioners agreed to sell to the Poles and a new scheme was approved by the Privy Council on 18 February 1981.

Over the next few months the church was cleaned and redecorated and as the Cardinal gave his blessing, St John's can never have been so full of proud parishioners since the day it was built.

ST FRANCIS XAVIER

In 1981 I saw no more wretched sight than the infamous Liverpool Piggeries, a cluster of high rise housing blocks not far from the centre of the city which were empty and appallingly vandalized. What was amazing was that the vandalism was not confined to the lower storeys, as high as a fiercely thrown brick might reach, but continued systematically floor by floor to the very top – some twenty storeys in all. Day after day, month after month, the whole neighbourhood must have echoed to the sound of breaking glass. All around was the same desolation – tarmac wastelands, broken pavements, and not a person, nor a car in sight. And this was a Wednesday afternoon at about 4 o'clock in August.

I was there not to see if the Piggeries could be saved (though a developer has now acquired them for renovation as flats) but to look at the great Roman Catholic church of St Francis Xavier nearby, one of the leading monuments to the revival and growth of Catholicism in the North during the nineteenth century. St Francis Xavier was under threat of demolition. Looking at the wasteland in which it stood, it was easy to imagine how the Church authorities might lose heart. Yet looked at another way the church was the only building in the area to suggest that a humane way of life had existed and could still exist. The whole church, including even the spire, was black with soot, yet it had immense presence and dignity. If it had houses and shops and pubs clustered around it instead of a wasteland created to provide breathing space for tower blocks it would be the focal point of an entire neighbourhood.

Yet surprisingly in view of all these problems St Francis Xavier still had a flourishing congregation. In April that year a petition against demolition bearing 8000 signatures had been handed to the Lord Mayor. Its future had become the subject of intense local argument.

The church had been built between 1845–49 by John Joseph Scoles. Though not a household name, he was the leading Catholic church architect of the first half of the nineteenth century after A.W.N. Pugin. His best known work is the sumptuous Jesuit church in Farm Street in Mayfair. He also designed churches in places as far afield as Bath, Birmingham and Great Yarmouth. Pugin had been obsessed with correctness, and reviving the mystery of medieval worship by strictly following medieval plans. At St Francis Xavier, Scoles used a variant of the classic counter Reformation plan familiar all over Europe in the seventeenth and eighteenth century – a broad nave, with a short raised chancel providing large congregations with a clear view of the High Altar. To improve the view from the aisles, the nave is supported on remarkably slender columns of polished Drogheda limestone. Thus, the whole decorative richness of the church can be taken in at a glance. On the south side, an exceptionally spacious and elaborate Sodality, or Lady Chapel, had been added in 1885–87 to designs of Edmund Kirby. Outside the presence of the church was greatly increased by the long train of buildings attached to it, culminating in the amazingly vigorous Campion School designed by Henry Clutton, the author of a volume on the *Domestic Architecture of France in the Middle Ages*. In 1875 Clutton had been appointed architect for the proposed Roman Catholic Cathedral at Westminster though this was eventually built to the designs of his pupil, J.F. Bentley. Clutton's interest in French Gothic found vigorous expression in the spectacular Flamboyant dormers, reminiscent of fifteenth-century town houses in France, carrying triangular gables set in pierced tracery panels, giving the school an immensely rich silhouette.

The church authorities' plan was to clear the site entirely, except for the church spire and the Sodality chapel, and to offer the land to a housing association. The Sodality chapel would be used for regular services but the main worship of the congregation, some 400 strong, would move to another church. As overtures to the church authorities had been unsuccessful, we wrote to Father Pedro Arrupe, the Superior General of the Jesuit order, and received a prompt and friendly reply only shortly before his death, appreciating SAVE's concern but emphasizing the scheme was part of a wider pastoral plan for the Catholic archdiocese of Liverpool as a whole. More alarmingly, we heard soon after that Liverpool City Corporation had accepted that the church could be demolished without listed building consent, because part of the building would continue in ecclesiastical use.

This was very disturbing news for a case in the House of Lords in 1974 concerning the Howard United Reformed Church in Bedford had established, definitively, that listed building consent was required for the total demolition of a listed church even if a new church was built on the site. The argument had revolved round a section in the Town and Country Planning Act of 1971, Section 56

ABOVE: The nave of St Francis Xavier in Liverpool. The Roman Catholic Archdiocese had decided to demolish the church apart from the tower and Sodality chapel. Public outcry and a threat of legal action prompted a change of plan.

(1) which provided an exemption "for works for the demolition . . . of . . . an ecclesiastical building which is for the time being used for ecclesiastical purposes or would be so used but for the works". The Law Lords had decided that where total demolition was concerned it could not be argued "the church would be so used but for the works" as clearly the church would no longer exist. This left the

position unresolved in cases such as St Francis Xavier where the body of the church was to be removed but a part retained for worship.

As neither the local authority nor the Department of the Environment was inclined to intervene, we decided to take action ourselves. Advised by Robert Carnwath, SAVE's solicitors, Gouldens sent a letter to the Archdiocesan Trustees on 14 August 1981 stating that in their view listed building consent was required and "the trustees would be committing a criminal offence if they proceeded with the works without consent". Gouldens reasoned that the Howard judgement "extends to the case where the demolition, although not total, is sufficiently substantial to alter or remove the identity of the building." "The chapel," they held, "represents no more than one sixth of the overall floor space and was a later addition. Even assuming a genuine ecclesiastical use of the chapel following demolition of the remainder, it cannot be said that *the church* as such is still in ecclesiastical use or would be but for the works." The reference in the Howard case to "partial demolition", the letter continued, "is in our view limited to works which leave the identity of the original building substantially intact." The letter asked for an assurance that the Trustees would not proceed with the proposals unless and until an application for listed building consent had been submitted and approved. The letter concluded, "Unless we received that assurance within 21 days, we have instructions to seek the leave of the Attorney General to bring proceedings for a declaration that listed building consent is required and an injunction." Two weeks later we received a letter from solicitors for the Archdiocese with the assurance we sought.

Then on 25 October came a public statement from the Archdiocese announcing that the plans for demolition had been withdrawn. "In the light of the strong feelings expressed in many quarters, and especially by parishioners, we propose that the church be kept whole and entire, and that such essential repairs be carried out as will allow it to remain in use." The Archdiocese was looking for financial help in carrying out repairs and here there were two sources of hope – the possibility of a substantial grant from the Historic Buildings Council and a newly-formed group of Friends of St Francis Xavier which could form a focus for fund raising. For a while there seemed little progress but nearly two years later, in October 1983, the long awaited news arrived in the form of a newsletter from the Friends that restoration had begun. The dry rot in the roof was being eradicated, valley gutters relined and new gutters and downspouts provided. As the roof is the priority with any building this was the news we had wanted.

In the 1981 statement the Archdiocese had still envisaged demolishing the adjoining buildings behind the church, which we very much wanted to see kept. Shortly after Merseyside County Council had taken them on for use for training schemes under the Manpower Service Commission, so the whole complex was now back in use.

There are a number of lessons to be drawn from this saga: the most effective campaign to save a major building is based on active local concern backed by strong support at national level. Secondly, even when a situation looks hopeless and the owners can see no way out but demolition, clear vigorous action can provide a solution that is acceptable to all parties, however much at loggerheads the two sides may be initially.

ALL SOULS, HALEY HILL

The story of All Souls shows that the whole Church system of dealing with redundant churches, while capable of coping with the main run of fine and historic churches, can seize up totally when a really outstanding building is faced with a huge repair problem. Nothing happens for months, and then years, while the problem and the figures involved become more and more frightening.

All Souls, an Anglican church on Haley Hill, Halifax was declared redundant in 1977 soon after a new minister had decided that the building was too much of a burden on the congregation and had moved services to the church hall. This was simply the first blow. The Diocese had then received an architect's report stating that the spire was in a dangerous condition and should be taken down as soon as possible and suggesting that rebuilding would cost not less than £200,000. The Historic Building Council had sent a deputation to look at the church consisting, we heard, of Sir John

Summerson, John Brandon Jones and J. Mordaunt Crook. They had concluded that the building did not merit the huge grant that would be needed to save it. The Church Commissioners' Advisory Board in their initial advice had not recommended "preservation" but alternative use and this means, to those who understand the coding, that if no alternative use could be found in the next three years they would concur in its demolition.

So why did we care? All Souls was to us a masterpiece, perhaps one of the dozen best Victorian churches in the country; the Victorian age being the greatest era of church building that Britain has seen since the Middle Ages. However, Sir George Gilbert Scott, its architect, had not been accorded a place in the pantheon of Victorian architectural genius. He was too prolific, and the boast that he had worked on more than 1000 churches counted against him. The stars of Burges, Butterfield, Bodley, Norman Shaw and Waterhouse had risen well above his. Scott's reputation still suffered from the taunt (quite untrue in fact) that he had taken his rejected Gothic design for the Foreign Office and used it virtually unchanged for the Midland Hotel at St Pancras Station. But by degrees his major buildings, St Pancras, the Foreign Office as built to his Renaissance design, the Albert Memorial, were being recognized as great buildings. The problem was, as Gavin Stamp pointed out, that while these buildings were all very much the product of their age, new building types incorporating new technology and planning, Scott's churches were self-consciously backward looking. He saw the great age of English church building as the late thirteenth century and his best churches sought to go back to that age, not to produce something new. He aimed to rival the great medieval spires of Grantham and Newark. He aspired to the finest craftsmanship. However, a church like All Souls was essentially an act of homage to what he regarded as the climax of great art and spirituality in church building. Yet, by degrees we are coming to see that great buildings do look back as well as forwards. Innovation is not the only measure of quality. Some of the most revered of Elizabethan country houses boast a medieval silhouette of battlements and towers, while the

OPPOSITE: All Souls, Haley Hill, Halifax, built in 1856–59 to the designs of Sir Gilbert Scott, was declared redundant in 1977.

backward look in the early twentieth century produced masterpieces like Lutyens' Castle Drogo.

All Souls was the product of a Montague and Capulet style rivalry between the two great mill-owning families in Halifax, the Crossleys and the Akroyds. The Crossleys were nonconformists and had paid for the 235 foot high spire of the handsome Congregational Church in the centre of the town which completely dominated Halifax's low-lying medieval parish church. The square Congregational Church, as it was known, was begun in 1855. The next year the Akroyds exhibited the design for Haley Hill at the Royal Academy. The church was to stand on a hill at the edge of the town with a great tower and spire soaring above the Crossley's spire in the valley below. Rivalry begat speed and All Souls was consecrated on 2 November 1859.

After three years of redundancy no one had come forward with a solution. Hopes that the Department of the Environment would take the church into guardianship, as it had done with a very select group of outstanding churches, including Burges's church in the park at Studley Royal in York, had foundered. The three years of the waiting period were up and when in November 1980 we heard that the Church Commissioners were calling a meeting at the church, we were sure that it was to set the seal on the fate of the building by demonstrating that there was no solution.

For in this case we were convinced that the usual solution for redundant churches of outstanding quality – vesting in the Redundant Churches Fund – would never be agreed by the Church Commissioners. The sums involved were too large. It was also an urban church and the Fund had been very reluctant to take on large town churches.

All Souls was the first major case faced by the northern office SAVE had established at Hebden Bridge in Yorkshire in 1978, and Ken Powell our northern secretary felt deeply that the building must be preserved at all costs. The problem was that All Souls was becoming an ever more disheartening sight. Some of the stained glass windows had been brutally vandalized. The windows had been boarded up so it was dark as well as dirty inside. Rain, too, was beginning to penetrate as slates slipped from the roof. The chill and dampness in summer as well as winter were depressing beyond belief. Yet one of the results of visiting so many empty buildings and later seeing them rescued and restored is that it breeds a determination not to be discouraged by appearances and to try all the harder to find a solution.

We produced a lightning leaflet *SAVE All Souls* on 14 November 1980 suggesting the formation of a new independent trust to take on the church and establish it as a major regional ecclesiastical museum. Sophie Andreae and Ken Powell took it to the meeting in the church and advocated the scheme sufficiently strongly for everyone there to examine it further. Suddenly things began to turn in our favour. Jennifer Jenkins, the chairman of the Historic Buildings Council, had become enthused by the church because of its immense townscape value. The Church Commissioners own Advisory Board of Redundant Churches indicated it would oppose demolition. The creation of the National Heritage Memorial Fund on 1 April 1980 offered a new source of funds if we could convince the trustees that All Souls was of national importance and that their support alone could save it. Soon after we found an architect willing to take on the church, initially on a wholly voluntary basis, and to prepare a properly phased plan. This was Donald Buttress who has made a speciality of church restoration. It was a lucky choice for us for once in harness Donald Buttress would speak with immense conviction and authority. Very soon we had the outline of a scheme: Phase I: a new temporary roof over the whole church to keep out water; Phase II: the tower and spire and Phase III: masonry repairs and permanent work on the roof. By showing how immediate action was possible while spreading the work over several years, we stood a better chance of winning over the funding bodies.

More detailed examinations showed that the stone work was in a less parlous condition than had been suggested, and repairs could be tackled over quite a long period. The idea had gained currency that Scott had used two incompatible stones which had reacted chemically against each other so, in Donald Sinden's memorable phrase (on a television programme filmed at the Church), All Souls was literally devouring itself. For all the surface decay in some places, Donald Buttress was able to show this was not really the case. Earlier reports had suggested that much of the tower must be taken down, but working with Ove Arups, he was able to argue for strengthening it *in situ*.

We now needed a body of supporters, so we decided to launch the Friends of All Souls, Haley Hill, and during a fortuitous lull in our skirmishes with British Rail, secured the use of Scott's stupendous staircase at St Pancras Station for the launch of the Friends on Saturday 5 December 1981. A Saturday was not perhaps the ideal day but the building was still partly in use as offices during the week and this was the venue we wanted. For Scott's staircase ranks among the most breathtaking I have ever seen, vying with the great baroque staircases of eighteenth century Germany in its combination of daring design and immensely rich colour and ornament.

The launch went well, we recruited nearly a hundred Friends but very soon after we were faced with the decision as to whether the Friends should take on the church. I went with John Maddison, vice chairman of the Friends, to seek the view of someone who had often advised us on tactics in such cases. "Under no circumstances take the church," he advised. "You're simply letting the Church Commissioners off the hook. If you win they'll be endlessly pressing you to take other redundant churches. If you fail they'll simply say 'we told you' and your credibility has gone. You have to force them to vest the church in the Redundant Churches Fund."

This was logical advice but I found it very depressing. I was sure this meant a very long fight during which the church would probably pass the point of no return. The question therefore was which did we put first – the building or the principle? Rapidly, it became clear that we had to proceed with the idea of a trust and here we had a very forceful ally in Michael Gillingham, a director of Sparks and a great expert on church organs – and indeed all things ecclesiastic. With the help of Herbert Robinson, the solicitor who had drawn up SAVE's trust deed, we set about establishing a Haley Hill Trust. On 3 June 1982 came the fateful day when a group of the trustees of the National Heritage Memorial Fund made a flying visit to Halifax to look at the church. We were left on tenterhooks as it was clear they were sharply divided. It was a beautiful day and this served to make the interior all the more gloomy. What church shut up for five years while the dirt accumulates and the rain soaks through can be anything else but profoundly dispiriting?

However, four months later, in October, we heard the glorious news. The National Heritage Memorial Fund had voted a grant to us of £250,000 towards the repair of the church and by the end of December we already had the contractors on site. The change when I went in January 1983 with Michael Gillingham was riveting. The interior had been cleared and tidied, the scaffolding was up, but it was not so much the physical change as the knowledge that at last we were in a position to do something. We no longer had to sit and watch while things went from bad to worse but were at last free to take direct action. Best of all was the pleasure of local residents that at last something was being done. Suddenly we found that the people living around really cared about the building and wanted to be kept in touch.

Now the finance was secure one crucial question remained, always first on everyone's lips. What are you going to do with the church? It was clear that there were major problems over our idea of

BELOW: Badly eroded stonework in the porch of All Souls.

an ecclesiastical museum. First of all there was the cost of installation, problems of security if the exhibits were of value and doubts as to whether we could attract loans of really interesting material. Even more than this was the potential conflict between the exhibits and the architecture of the interior. All Souls was a building which needed to be kept intact and admired for its own qualities. Yet it was equally clear we could not simply install a ticket booth and expect people to come on guided tours. It was then that a memory of a visit to Schwetzingen in southern Germany planted an idea in my mind. Schwetzingen is most famous for its remarkable garden, filled with exotic buildings including a spectacular Moorish pavilion. When I had visited the Schloss we had been taken to the very pretty rococo theatre and had sat down to watch, for twelve minutes or so, a delightful spectacle consisting of a series of automated scene changes accompanied by recorded music. It was very simple but enchantingly done and all the more memorable because it was so unusual.

At All Souls we had the pews, or most of them, and I began to wonder whether we could not bring parties of visitors and seat them in the pews and tell them something, not about the church but about churchmanship and the style of worship it was built to serve and proclaim. The Church has so much spectacular music and liturgy, such a range of nuances from high Anglican to low Evangelical. A dramatically presented programme with recorded voices and music, principally serious and thought provoking but occasionally light-hearted and witty, might reveal far more about the purpose the church was built to serve than a normal visit to a church ever could.

By mid-summer in 1983 All Souls had a new roof visible from all over Halifax. The interior had been cleared and cleaned and the churchyard made presentable once again. Work on the tower and spire is scheduled to begin in 1984 and once this is done the trust can set to work on the greatest challenge of all – bringing the church to life again.

LIGHTCLIFFE

When SAVE Britain's Heritage came into being early in 1975, European Architectural Heritage Year, one of the first cases we took up was a beautiful Victorian church in Lightcliffe, Yorkshire. A local resident, Mrs Barbara Allan, telephoned SAVE's first secretary Sarah Seymour in March to ask for our help. By chance it was at the end of March 1982, seven years later, that the church was reopened, restored and adapted to a most unexpected new use. The story of Lightcliffe is a classic example of the way one determined individual, with persistence, can keep the fight going long enough for a solution, satisfactory to all sides, to emerge. And Mrs Allan's fight was all the more remarkable as she was undergoing treatment for cancer at the time.

Lightcliffe is an attractive and leafy village on the A58 as it approaches Halifax from the east, full of handsome Victorian villas surrounded by banks of rhododendrons. The parish church of St Matthew dating from 1874 is dignified but inconspicuous and nearby is the pathetic remnant of the Georgian church built by a Halifax mason, William Mallinson, in 1775. This once had a fine box-pewed interior but had stood empty and a prey to vandals for so long that in the end the Church authorities decided that only the tower could be preserved. This now stands awkwardly in a trim square graveyard. Higher up the hill in a much more prominent position stands the Congregational Church with a proud spire that dominates the whole village. Here was certainly a case where nonconformists wished to show that they were the leading denomination in the district. At first sight, in fact, the Lightcliffe United Reformed Church, as it had become following the union of the Congregationalists with the Presbyterian Church of England in 1972, looks like the parish church, with a soaring tower and spire to catch the eye of every passer-by. The church had been built in 1871 to the designs of the great Bradford partnership, Lockwood and Mawson, whose work included Bradford's memorable town hall, the stupendous Manningham Mills and more unexpectedly the Civil Service Stores in London. The site had been bought by John Crossley of Crossley's Carpets, who had built the spectacular Congregational

church in Halifax's town centre. The first £2,000 had been contributed by Sir Titus Salt, builder of the model industrial estate at Saltaire and its Congregational church. Salt's daughters had laid the foundation stone and put in three handsome stained glass windows, one facing south towards the Salt estate. The main stained glass window in the west end, the Titus Salt Memorial Window, had been installed by his business associates and workers.

In September 1974 plans had been published for the demolition of the church and its replacement by a new multi-purpose worship centre. Mrs Allan had organized a petition and on 24 October had succeeded in getting the church listed by the Department of the Environment. The Church authorities had nonetheless applied for consent to demolish and this time for permission to erect eight flats and garages on the site. What really rankled with local residents was the fact that just a few years earlier in September 1971 the church had celebrated its centenary and "thousands of pounds were collected and spent on redecorating, cleaning all the interior stone work, and generally putting the place in sound condition". Mrs Allan continued, "There are absolutely no repairs needed on this magnificent building, so you can imagine how local people are feeling at the prospect of all the money that was spent going to waste."

Following the press release SAVE issued, BBC's *Look North* team arrived to film the church. "The filming was absolutely magnificent," Mrs Allan reported. "They had taken shots from every angle, and even gone further out into the area to show the church in its surroundings . . . it was a gorgeous day, so consequently the film showed the church to full advantage." For three years there was stalemate then in 1978 the Church authorities applied again for consent to demolish: this was refused on the casting vote of the Chairman on 15 November after a debate of over an hour. Mrs Allan had again been instrumental in saving the church – this time by developing an alternative scheme for using the church as a parish museum and craft centre, towards which the Landmark Trust had generally given £1,000 as seed money. This contribution was to lead

OPPOSITE: The United Reformed Church at Lightcliffe near Halifax came under threat in 1975 soon after it had been restored for its centenary. Determined opposition delayed demolition until a viable alternative appeared. The church has now become a flourishing craft emporium.

ABOVE: Shopping under the eaves of the former Lightcliffe United Reformed Church.

to a solution; the transformation of the church into the Real-Stone Working Craft Centre which opened on 31 March 1982.

Now parties arrive by busload to visit the church. Externally, it is virtually unaltered except for a change of noticeboard on the road. Internally the transformation is remarkable: more drastic perhaps than might be wished in a building of quality, but sufficiently ingenious to be intriguing, and so successful in terms of bringing life to the building that at the end I felt positively thankful. The ingenuity lies in the amount of space created. It is always difficult in a shopping emporium to lure people upstairs or downstairs, away from the main floor. Here it is done by a series of half levels, so that you continually catch a glimpse of what is happening above and eventually arrive at a cafe immediately beneath the arches of the nave. As far as possible the internal features have been retained, providing unexpectedly close encounters with windows and mouldings that would normally only be seen from below. In all there are more than a dozen shops and stalls, and some thirty people work in the church.

It must be a matter of personal taste what you make of the wares on sale, but there is no doubt that the Lightcliffe United Reformed Church is one of the country's more unusual church conversions.

ST MARK'S, NORTH AUDLEY STREET

One of the sadder sights in Mayfair in recent years has been the elegant Ionic portico of St Mark's, North Audley Street. The front is flush with neighbouring buildings and at first glance it is not even obvious that it is a church – the octagonal lantern surmounted by a cross is set back behind the parapet and only visible from across the street. The whole front consists simply of a giant portico, rising to the height of the second floor of neighbouring buildings. The reason it is often passed unnoticed is that it has a portico *in antis*; a recessed, not a projecting portico like the nearby Grosvenor Chapel or St George's, Hanover Square. The detail is chastely Greek, not Roman, as befits the architect, J.P. Gandy-Deering, who had travelled to Greece and Asia Minor in 1811–13 on behalf of the Society of Dilettanti – to which he was elected in 1830. He had taken the name of Deering in 1828 on inheriting an estate from his friend Henry Deering and from this time had gradually relinquished architecture for the pursuits of a country gentleman. His London buildings have almost all been demolished and his most familiar building is the unusual Grecian front of the former Pimlico Literary Institution in Ebury Street where Ian Fleming, creator of James Bond, used to live.

The portico of St Mark's is the most elegant and sophisticated surviving example of his work. However, in recent years it has become tatty through neglect, even being used as a dump for unwanted rubbish. While it was still in use as a parish church it had doubled for some considerable time as the American church in London. Being so close to the United States embassy in Grosvenor Square its location was ideal. When it became clear that St Marks was to be declared redundant, the American congregation had naturally tried to buy it – offering, I was told by their minister, "two hundred thousand bucks". The offer was not accepted – the reason, I gathered, being that the Diocese of London had had a much higher offer, approaching half a million pounds, from a developer. He had proposed creating a shopping arcade, or emporium, inside the church, and on an autumn afternoon in 1978 he arranged for a group from SAVE to visit the church so he could explain the scheme.

Inside Gandy-Deering's portico is an unusual hall – a version of the Greek *pronaos*, a vestibule before the sanctuary. The church itself, however, had been entirely rebuilt by Sir Arthur Blomfield in 1878 with a colourful Gothic interior in complete contrast with the Regency entrance. Blomfield's work is not rated very highly today, but the interior of St Mark's was wonderfully rich with very fine fittings. The Diocese of London had served notice that most of these fittings were to be removed – the memorials on the walls; the doorcase into the nave; the font; the pulpit and all the fittings of the chancel, including the splendid organ and organ case; the choir stalls; the altar and retable. The developer told us his scheme was based on suppressing all evidence that the building was once a church and that he wanted to insert a false ceiling concealing Blomfield's fine and bold timber roof over the nave.

We subsequently wrote objecting to the proposal in the strongest terms, stating that we thought the best use was continuing ecclesiastical use, pointing to the nearby Ukranian Catholic Cathedral of the Holy Family in Exile. This now flourished in a former congregational church in Duke Street, built in 1889–91 to the design of Alfred Waterhouse, the architect of the Natural History Museum. At the same time, to try and demonstrate a sympathetic alternative use was possible, we put in a parallel application for change of use to a 'Heritage Centre'. Our idea was that the church could be used as an auditorium or lecture hall with very little change to its character other than the removal of pews. It might be possible for example to put a glass screen between nave and chancel, and arrange the lighting so that when the body of the church was lit, the chancel was dark and more or less invisible. However, should the chancel be required, it could be lit and visually united with the church. I have seen a glass screen of this kind rising the full height of the Ägidienkirche in Lübeck, sealing off the east end so that it could

OPPOSITE: The chaste Greek Revival portico of St Mark's, North Audley Street in London's Mayfair. Though it was to be declared redundant, London refused to sell the church to the American congregation which had held services there.

be heated separately in winter; and because it was glass, and sensitively inserted in an arch, it did not interfere with the lines of the architecture. We felt that such a hall or auditorium could also be let for conferences generating revenue, and be available for community uses in the evening. The *pronaos* provided just the kind of hall or foyer needed for such uses. In addition, there was an attractive paved yard shaded by a large tree to the north of the building which could be used for outdoor gatherings. On one side of the yard were a group of former school buildings, now very decrepit, which could have been repaired, or if necessary rebuilt to provide ancillary accommodation such as a dining hall and kitchen. With the help of Max Hanna of the English Tourist Board we established there was a demand for this type of medium-sized conference hall seating 100 – 200 people in the centre of London. Then we discovered another piece of good news: the crypt was currently leased as a recording studio at a rent of £10,000-a-year and the tenant was keen to renew.

On 29 March 1979, Westminster Planning Committee rejected the Diocese's application to convert St Mark's to a shopping emporium but agreed in principle to our proposal for a heritage centre. The Diocesan authorities, understandably perhaps, were extremely annoyed with us, and initially were very reluctant to discuss the matter at all. However, Piers Rodgers, a Mayfair resident (and now Secretary of the Royal Academy) undertook to explore the matter and worked out an intriguing proposal whereby St Mark's might be used by the nearby Montessori School, releasing other buildings currently zoned for educational use, as offices. This would have involved a complicated three-way exchange between the Diocese, the Grosvenor Estate and the educational tenant. We asked Clutton's to explore the idea further but when they asked the agents of the Diocese for a meeting, they met with a refusal.

The Diocese in the meantime had produced a new brief, requiring the church should be left largely intact, and placed it on the market in March 1983 on this basis. Several offers of the order of half a million pounds were received – which appeared to show that the character of the church could be preserved and the Diocese receive a worthwhile return – but the use of the church remains a very live issue. The local Montessori school has sponsored a petition opposing a plan to turn the church into a restaurant. The battle continues.

AMERSFOORT

St John's Reading and St Francis Xavier in Liverpool were both examples where it was possible for the church to continue in ecclesiastical use in a wholly appropriate way. But the majority of redundant churches, if they are to survive, have to find a totally new use. Several have been very successfully adapted for cultural and community activities but in every case this depends on the need being there and money from public or charitable sources being forthcoming. Faced with so many redundant churches, the challenge is increasingly to find other sympathetic uses which are financially viable – where, to put it simply, the money put into buying, repairing and adapting the building is covered by an increase in value, so that if it is sold, costs can be recouped.

With many historic buildings residential use is the answer. People will pay a capital sum for the completed houses or flats, and residential use brings people who will appreciate and enjoy the qualities of the building and its setting. With a church the situation is different. First, the idea of a church becoming a house may upset local residents, particularly if the churchyard has been used recently for burials. Some individuals and groups, the Friends of Friendless Churches, for example, have very strong objections in principle to the use of a consecrated building for domestic purposes. Architecturally, too, it presents great problems. For the quality of most churches lies in the fact that they are continuous flowing open spaces, and any attempt to subdivide them internally by partitions, galleries or inserted floors conflicts with their character. I have encountered one or two very minimal conversions of churches as houses – where the interior has been left virtually intact and become one large studio-living room with perhaps a kitchen or bathroom installed in a vestry or under the gallery. But this is still anathema to those who object to the idea in principle. Where a church interior has been radically subdivided to make rooms and passages as in a normal house the results can be very painful.

As sometimes happens, one building, beautifully converted, gave me the answer to the question. This was the Elleboog church in the Dutch town of Amersfoort. I had gone to Holland in July 1977 shortly after the opening of the Victoria and Albert churches exhibition to look at churches converted to alternative uses. The problem of redundancy was nearly as marked as in England – but due not so much to a decline in church-going but a shift of population to the suburbs. This was affecting Victorian churches in city centres and one of the revelations of the visit was to find some really stupendous nineteenth century churches, in a very distinctive Gothic.

We went to the Round Lutheran Church, Amsterdam, with an interior dating from 1822 built on a circular plan with giant columns carrying two tiers of encircling galleries. It had been disused as long ago as 1935 but recently had become a conference hall attached to the new Sonesta Hotel. The floor was filled with parents watching a children's tap dancing competition, but the combination of plush hotel carpeting, and self-consciously placed baskets of flowers seemed out of place beneath the cool white colonnade and dome.

The next day we went to Amersfoort and there I saw what to me is still the best example I have seen of a contemporary use and a modern interior inserted in an old church. The interior of the Elleboog church is neo-classical at its coolest and cleanest – a barrel vaulted nave carried on Ionic colonnades with walls, columns and aisle ceilings all in white. The church had become an open-plan architects' office but all the clutter and furniture of the office beneath had been neatly separated from the architecture above by the introduction of a lighting grid. Below all was colour and activity. Above, nothing disturbed the architectural lines of the building. The large lofty evenly-lit space proved ideal, I was told, for studio-work, and, in laying out the areas for people to work in, the designer had ordered them very much following the blocks of pews, so you still walked formally up the aisles and across the nave at right angles. Order and harmony had thus been brought by line and colour – bright greens and reds predominating.

HEADINGLEY HILL

Amersfoort was an ideal but the problem is always to translate a success seen abroad into action at home. The problem was particularly acute in Yorkshire, where Ken Powell, SAVE's Northern secretary, was working on a report on northern nonconformist chapels – *The Fall of Zion*, published in the summer of 1980. But fortunately there was one really encouraging success. At Headingley in Leeds, the Headingley Hill United Reformed Church had been a problem for some time. The congregation had sought consent to demolish it, but this had been rejected, but no solution had been in sight until it had been suddenly acquired by a design firm with the unusual name of Bulldog.

The Headingley Hill chapel was the work of Cuthbert Brodrick, the architect of Leeds's spectacular Town Hall. Brodrick, in my view, is one of unsung geniuses of Victorian architecture – he deserves to be much more of a household name. But his practice was entirely in the north and like Francis Smith of Warwick or Thomas Harrison of Chester, he never designed a building in London. Thus he has been regarded as a provincial with the dismissive overtures that implies. Brodrick had begun as pupil and assistant of the great Bradford architect Henry Lockwood, and had travelled on the

BELOW: The Elleboog Church at Amersfoort in Holland. A beautiful neoclassical church transformed into architects' offices without damage to the original architecture.

continent settling in France to paint after his retirement. Brodrick's works included the Grand Hotel at Scarborough and the deliciously exotic city baths at Leeds, a moorish fantasy that alas no longer survives.

The Headingley Hill chapel, built as a Congregational Church in 1862–64, stands on the main road to Ilkley surrounded by substantial Victorian villas. Like so many northern city churches, it is jet black, and all the more imposing for it. Brodrick had to build on steeply rising ground so he designed a broad grand staircase, such as one might find in Rome, up to the entrance doors – twin doors, in a single arch, which echo the nonconformist tradition of separate entrances and seating for men and women. Over the entrance is an immense rose window; to the right a round tower carrying an unusual lozenge-shaped spire. To give the flanks of the church greater interest Brodrick placed gables over all the windows, with

BELOW: Headingley Hill United Reform Church in Leeds. After an application for listed building, consent to demolish was refused. It was sold as an open plan office and successfully adapted.

roofs running back at right angles to the main roof over the nave.

Walking inside on a cold wintery morning, used to the usual dark chill atmosphere of an empty church in November, the transformation was startling. The church was ablaze with light, warm and full of people working, yet the interior was intact. Bulldog was using the building as it stood, as open-plan offices. The pews had been taken out but the rest of the woodwork remained – the gallery over the entrance, the organcase behind the platform from which the minister had conducted services. Bulldog's outlay, we were told, had been some £40,000, including £15,000 for the purchase of the building. The question which immediately springs to mind is, but what are the heating bills. The answer was simple, no more than in Bulldog's previous offices where they were all working in separate rooms which had to be heated individually.

In January 1983 I went back to the church. Bulldog had sold the building on to Gillinson Barret and Partners, a large architectural practice working in Leeds. There were now more people working in the building and further work had been carried out, making the whole internal arrangement more formal. A new heating system had been installed – gas reflectors suspended from the roof beams which had reduced the heating bill from £100 a week to £40. Following further improvements the capital value of the building had recently been put at £216,000, a substantial increase on the £15,000 Bulldog had paid a few years before. Examining these heaters from the vantage point of the gallery at the back of the church provided another glimpse of Broderick's highly individual approach to design. The slender cast iron columns carried not conventional arches but highly complex pieces of carpentry, a little akin, in miniature, to the structure of the early timber railway viaducts. These were treated with bold semi-circular notches – suggestive of the workings of a watch on a giant scale – both evidence of Brodrick's desire to work out every detail *de novo*.

ST JAMES, GUERNSEY

On a Bank Holiday Monday in 1982 I was invited to make the short flight from Jersey to Guernsey to attend a party being given in aid of

St James Church. The story of St James is an instance of just how much persistence is needed to devise and implement a rescue plan for a church – in this case ten years at least.

St James in fact, was one of the restoration projects put forward for European Architectural Heritage Year in 1975, but by the end of the year nothing whatsoever had happened. By degrees the lobby to demolish it grew, and a proposal was drawn up to build a new police station on the site, preserving just the portico.

"A box with a phoney Greek temple in front and a pepperpot on top" was one verdict on St James but to my mind it is a building of some considerable distinction. It stands towards the top of the hill above St Peter Port, the island's capital, surrounded by quiet pleasant streets of Regency houses – almost all in stucco, painted today in pretty pastel colours with good ironwork railings and balconies. St James is also in stucco – or more precisely the Roman cement sometimes favoured by neo-classical architects in preference even to stone. The Grange in Hampshire was in Roman cement, and one of the attractions of the material was that it gave, when properly used, a very clear even surface and a superbly crisp edge to all the architectural mouldings. It is the perfect material for fluted Greek Doric columns – as are used on both the Grange and St James. The use of Roman cement can also make the columns look as if they are cut from a single shaft of stone. Part of the beauty of St James was the colour of the Roman cement – not a cold grey but a wonderful warm honey colour like the best Bath stone, so that on a clear day the whole building positively glows.

The church was built as a thanksgiving for the Victory at Waterloo. The project was conceived at a meeting on 30 October 1815, just four months and twelve days after the battle, under the inspiration of Admiral Sir James Saumarez, the naval commander who had played a major role in maintaining the blockade of France throughout the Napoleonic Wars.

Work began on 3 August 1816 and the church was consecrated two years later, almost to the day, on 16 August 1818. The architect was John Wilson, who designed a number of prominent public buildings on the island including the Markets in 1822, as well as numerous private houses. Like his contemporary, William Wilkins, who designed the National Gallery in London, and the Gothic screen at King's College, Cambridge, he designed in Gothic as well as Greek – his Elizabeth College, which looks over St James is in a very handsome Tudor Gothic. Howard Colvin in his *Dictionary of British Architects* notes that one of Wilson's drawings for a Place d'Armes in Alderney is in the distinctive style of the Royal Engineers, and this may explain Wilson's sudden departure from Guernsey in 1830 – a John Wilson was Clerk of the Works at the Royal Arsenal, Woolwich from 1839 to 1843.

In style and form St James is very akin to the so-called Waterloo Churches in England, built following an Act of Parliament in 1818 in a bid to combat the growth of nonconformity. The best of these are by Nash and Soane: what is interesting is that St James predates the British Act of Parliament and the Waterloo Commissioners' Churches it most resembles – such as St George's, Brandon Hill in Bristol, and St Anne's, Wandsworth in London which both date from the early 1820s.

St James was built as a garrison church where the British soldiers could attend services in English; at the time worship in the main church in town was conducted in French. Inside it is interesting to find it is similar in form to another garrison church, the Dockyard chapel at Chatham built in 1808–11. Both are large broad preaching boxes, with horseshoe balconies: St James seated 1300 people. I had been asked to support the campaign to save St James by writing an article for the *Guernsey Evening Post*, showing how other empty churches in Britain had been successfully restored and adapted to new uses by local people – and there were several close parallels. Holy Trinity, Maidstone dating from 1826–28, was being converted as a cultural centre. In Edinburgh the Greek Revival Church of Newington St Leonard had been brilliantly transformed as a concert hall. Such precedents were appropriate: a survey published in November 1981 has suggested that no less than 35 organizations in Guernsey representing thousands of islanders would use St James for 235 days each year for concerts, youth activities, exhibitions, meetings, lectures and debates.

The Friends of St James subsequently offered to lease the church from the States of Jersey, depositing £40,000 with the States

as a guarantee. On 1 December 1983 the States of Guernsey voted to spend £458,000 to restore and adapt the church as a concert hall. Work is scheduled to take eighteen months and is due for completion in 1985, European Music Year – eleven years behind the original target but nonetheless an achievement worth fighting for all the way.

OPPOSITE: St James Church in St Peter Port, Guernsey. This handsome Regency church, built to commemorate the Battle of Waterloo, stood empty and under threat for more than ten years. Following a prolonged battle it is being converted into a concert hall.

TERRACE & TOWN HOUSES

ON THURSDAY 20 JANUARY 1977 *The Times* carried a photograph showing a row of policemen standing shoulder to shoulder to prevent protesters from entering St Agnes Place in Lambeth. Behind them a large mobile crane was progressing down the street wielding a ball and chain, smashing in the fronts of houses one after another. The aim was simple: to do sufficient damage to every house in the street in the shortest possible time and thus to ensure it was quite impractical to renovate them. Lambeth Council knew an injunction was likely to be served that morning to halt demolition, so the cranes moved in at dawn with a guard of more than 200 police. The hope was that the whole street would be beyond repair before the courts opened. As it happened the judge granted an injunction in chambers and demolition was stopped when just eleven of the twenty-six target houses in the street had been wrecked. On the following Sunday the police officer commanding the force present at the demolition, Commander Patrick Flynn of L division, was quoted in *The Sunday Times* as saying: "I don't want to be involved in anything like this again. We are not street politicians."

I tell this story because it shows the lengths to which local authorities will go to destroy traditional streets of often attractive housing which, even if in poor condition, could well be improved to modern standards. In European Architectural Heritage Year, 1975, SAVE unearthed the statistic that 60 to 75 per cent of the housing demolished by the Greater London Council between 1967 and 1971 was in fair to good condition and could have been rehabilitated. In

OPPOSITE: Shepherdess Walk, Hackney, London, a delightful row of small late Georgian houses which came under threat in 1975. Following a vigorous local and national campaign they have been repaired and reoccupied.

ABOVE: Policemen in St Agnes Place, Lambeth, London, protecting demolition cranes sent in by the Borough Council on 19 January 1977 to destroy a street of Victorian terrace houses against powerful local opposition. Hours afterwards, the work was halted by a court injunction.

some Labour areas small terrace houses were demolished regardless of their condition because renovation would simply mean "more liberal votes" as one Hackney Councillor bluntly told a visiting conservationist. But Conservative councils have often pursued exactly the same policies and proved just as inflexible and bigoted in their attitudes. The name of the game was, of course, slum clearance.

While some areas of older housing were certainly beyond redemption, many others could have been improved and provided with sanitation, hot water, damp proofing, not only far more cheaply but far more quickly than replacement houses could ever have been built. But clearance was indiscriminatory – houses were condemned as at the end of their useful life when people were living in them and wanting to stay there. Any examination of local authority papers on housing in years to come will show this phrase "at the end of its useful life" appearing again and again. Once this verdict had been passed a building was condemned. Yet what does it mean? The term "at the end of its useful life" begs the question of useful to whom? In almost every case where buildings have been demolished under this catch-all phrase, there are other buildings nearby of similar date and construction which have survived and been successfully renovated. Buildings do not have a specific lifespan which can be defined in advance – much depends on the quality of maintenance over the years. When they need major repairs or improvements this can often still be cheaper and more satisfactory than replacement. Modern buildings, it is true are often required to have a certain minimum lifespan – say 30 to 60 years: what happened in some cases was that the council officials interpreted these lifespans as the maximum for existing buildings.

Behind it all lay a much more sinister and draconian piece of social engineering on a scale hardly seen even in Communist countries. The kernel of this philosophy was expressed most succinctly by the planner Wilfred Burns in *New Towns for Old* in 1963: "One result of slum clearance is that a considerable movement of people takes place over long distances, with devastating effect on the social grouping built up over the years. But, one might argue, this is a good thing when we are dealing with people who have no initiative or civic pride. The task, surely, is to break up such groupings even though the people seem to be satisfied with their miserable environment and seem to enjoy an extrovert social life in their own locality."

One result of these policies was, of course, the tower blocks which have brought misery to millions. Every week brings news of more high rise housing that is condemned. As I write on 12 November 1983, *The Times* carries a report "Tenants appeal for demolition of estate" telling the story of an estate of tower blocks in Hackney which have been faulty and damp since they were built sixteen years ago. The cost of repairs to the seven tower blocks, each containing 80 flats, and the 117 low rise houses (which the tenants also want to see demolished) to a good standard would be £27 million.

Poor design and construction are usually cited as the cause of problems but the more general point against most of these estates that needs to be made is that they are conceived and laid out as ghettoes. Ghetto is an emotive term but by definition a ghetto is a quarter of a town set apart for certain people to live in. The classic modern housing estate has no public roads through it, few people go there except those who live there, and the tragedy is that as vandalism increases some of the occupants are more and more afraid of venturing out of their homes. The traditional pattern of streets has a familiarity to all: in an estate of tower blocks even a policeman often finds it impossible to describe on his radio precisely where he is.

If all this was past history it might have no place here: the problem is that housing clearance is still far too often being pursued with the same blinkered zeal as it was in the 1950s and 1960s.

SAVE's first battle of this kind was over Shepherdess Walk in Hackney. This was a handsome terrace of 29 two-storey houses all of which had recently been listed. They were engagingly modest in scale but had an individuality as a result of a kink two thirds of the way along the terrace. The ground floors were stuccoed with windows and doors set in arched recesses, and the first floor sash windows opened onto very pretty iron balconies. Most of the houses had been emptied and boarded up to keep out squatters and the council wanted to demolish the terrace to extend a small park for local residents. However, the park was hardly worthy of the name – a flat stretch of grass, it seemed little used, with a few wispy, very young trees held up by stakes – which only added to the desolation of the area. And all around were other clusters of boarded up houses – fragments of terraces which were now empty and awaiting demolition. There was a vigorous local campaign developing against the demolition of 9–67 Shepherdess Walk. Guy Jervis, Chairman of the Hackney Society, estimated that the houses could be renovated at a cost of £10,000 each. This was at a time when the average two bedroom council flat in London was costing £30,000 and Hackney was spending up to £50,000 on such flats.

Public outcry saved Shepherdess Walk and three years later the houses were under scaffolding and being repaired by a housing association.

ABOVE: The terrace in Shepherdess Walk, Hackney, after restoration.

THE TRIANGLE

We had less good fortune – though an equally strong case – with a remarkable model housing layout in Merthyr Tydfil in Wales, known as the Triangle. Merthyr Tydfil Borough Council had decided to celebrate European Architectural Heritage Year in a unique way, by applying on 25 February 1975, for consent to demolish all but two of the town's eighty listed buildings. Most of these were in The Triangle, which consisted of three terraces of two-storey houses laid out around a green, and built between 1840 and 1852 for Anthony Hill of the Plymouth Ironworks in the town. Like most such housing, they were very modest, but the houses were larger than many of their kind, with a window on either side of the front door. It was claimed they were surrounded by local industry – the Hoover factory was just across the road, though this fell victim to the recession, when its closure was announced in 1981.

However, as the houses looked onto the green, and had small walled front gardens overlooking the grass, the whole triangle was turned in on itself, and potentially very secluded.

Due to public outcry, the houses survived Heritage Year. The local Civic Society produced a rehabilitation scheme showing how they could be brought up to current official housing standards providing housing for 145 people at a total cost of £350,000. An inquiry began on 3 December 1975 and by this time there was vigorous local opposition with support from Plaid Cymru, the Welsh Nationalist Party. The Inspector concluded in his report that the Triangle and other adjoining houses in Church Street had "considerable architectural interest on account of their group value and the unique nature of their layout; they are also of some historic interest". Nor did the land use considerations, in his opinion, override the case for preservation. "The adjoining industrial buildings

BELOW: The Triangle at Merthyr Tydfil in South Wales. This remarkable, and intact, model layout of mid-19th-century workers' housing has been demolished.

are not unduly obtrusive and do not appear to have given rise to complaints in the past, nor does there appear to be an established need to develop the site for industrial purposes." The Civic Society, he accepted "have demonstrated that an attractive and practicable scheme of rehabilitation is possible. Although the evidence suggests that this might be more costly to the ratepayers than renewal I am not satisfied that the additional cost would be as high as is suggested by the Council". For these good reasons the Inspector recommended refusal of listed building consent to the Triangle and the houses in Church Street but this was not acceptable to the Welsh Office and the Secretary of State for Wales. He agreed that the buildings were of considerable architectural interest but was swayed by the fact that in May 1974 he had accepted the conclusions of one of his inspectors that all the buildings "*had come to the end of their useful lives and were not suitable for retention and improvement*" (my italics). The fact that the Civic Society's scheme *might* be more costly to the rate-payers than renewal led him to conclude that: "in present economic circumstances . . . a sufficiently strong case has not been made out to preserve the buildings." And so, the Triangle, for all its interest and potential charm as a place to live was demolished.

QUARRY HILL

In the summer of 1976, while looking at redundant churches in Leeds with Peter Burman and Ken Powell, I went to look at the blackened but still noble St Mary's, Quarry Hill, a Commissioners' church of 1823–25 built by Thomas Taylor. He had worked for eight years for James Wyatt before settling in Leeds about 1805. The cause of redundancy, as elsewhere in Leeds, was immediately apparent: demolition of housing and loss of local residents. In this case the housing was still there, awaiting demolition – not nineteenth century back to backs but the great complex known as the Quarry Hill Flats, designed in 1935 and completed six years later.

When built it was the largest estate in England, and one of the landmarks of the modern movement in Britain. Its long sinuous blocks brought to mind Le Corbusier's famous plan for the City of Algiers. It seems, in fact, that the City Corporation and its architect R.A.H. Livett, who was then employed by Manchester, were

ABOVE: Quarry Hill Flats, Leeds in 1978 awaiting demolition. Architecturally, it was one of the most acclaimed examples of the Modern Movement in the 1930s.

principally influenced by recent municipal housing they had seen in Vienna and Berlin, notably K. Eyn's Karl-Seitz-Hof in Vienna built in 1927–30. From outside the Quarry Hill flats were impressive yet forbidding, the grimmer because of the traffic swirling past on new dual carriageways. Yet once inside, through the huge elliptical entrance arches, we were in an oasis. The great curving walls of the flats were a barrier to all the noise of the city, and the gardens inside were full of mature trees and shrubs. The seven-storey blocks no longer seemed intimidating but stylish – with the streamlined look of much of the best 1930s design. Yet the flats were completely empty. Here, but a short time ago hundreds of families could have lived. Now weeds were choking the neat brick walks in the pavements, doors were boarded up and the first windows had been broken. Yet the vandalism was still surprisingly slight – little graffiti and as yet none of the abandoned junk and debris that usually collects on such a site.

In one sense Quarry Hill stood for everything that people have come to despise in municipal housing – but standing there in such peace and in such pleasant gardens, destruction on such a scale seemed a waste. I learnt more of the background a year later from Randolph Langenbach who included a discussion of the destruction of Quarry Hill in a dissertation he had written at the York Institute of Advanced Architectural Studies. On the surface Randolph wrote: "the reason for its demolition seems quite simple and unassailable. The flats were constructed in an experimental system of steel and concrete originated by Eugene Mopin in France during the 1920s. Because of a combination of mistakes in the design and application of the system, together with delays and problems during the construction, the exterior pre-cast slabs proved not to be very durable, and water began to attack the steel frame, seriously weakening what was already a very light structure". Over the next twenty-five years maintenance costs were higher than on other Leeds housing estates, and the point was reached in the 1960s where £2 million had to be spent on permanent repairs, or £500,000 giving the estate no more than a further 15 years life! The second solution was chosen because of "the age of the estate". From there on Quarry Hill was run down, even before the demolition plans were finally announced in 1973. No champions entered the lists for the preservation of the Quarry Hill flats and they were entirely demolished about a year later.

GEORGIAN DUBLIN

In October 1978 I was invited to Dublin where consideration was being given to the formation of an Irish Committee of ICOMOS, the International Council on Monuments and Sites. I was secretary of the British Committee of ICOMOS at the time and this was my first visit to Dublin. Looking round the city on a brilliantly clear winter day I was astonished to find how beautiful it was – its beauty lying in continuity and coherence – with still unbelievable sequences of Georgian streets and squares both north and south of the River Liffey. The fronts of these houses are often plainly treated without even a simple cornice at the top but collectively they have a wonderful patina. Rarely do two fronts have brickwork of exactly the same colour and texture – different tints of pink and red and brown constantly abut, sometimes with a change of brick halfway up a facade. Thanks to Dublin's clean air the brickwork has retained its original colour, softened only slightly by the mellowness of age. But behind these plain fronts are fine Georgian interiors far more numerous than can be found in London. House after house has plasterwork of virtuoso quality – baroque, rococo and neo-classical, all equally dazzling and accomplished.

The most remarkable houses I saw on that visit were those in Henrietta Street – a street of houses, in the words of Maurice Craig's *Dublin*: "of so palatial a cast that one easily understands how it remained the most fashionable single street in Dublin till the Union, long after many rival centres of social attraction had been created." In 1792 an Archbishop, two bishops and four MPs were living in Henrietta Street, but subsequently some of the houses had endured almost a century of neglect. We went round No. 13 where a young couple had just moved in and were planning to restore the house by degrees. It was an astonishing sight, paint flaking from the ceiling, bare panelling showing telltale signs where partitions had been removed and a great hollow space where the main staircase had once stood. Yet at the same time it was remarkably complete, fine panelling, handsome doors, marble chimneypieces and cornices, and even full entablatures survived in room after room. Three of the houses had been bought by an architect noted for his interest in conservation but others were empty and one had been badly damaged by fire.

This trip brought me into contact with Kevin Nowlan and Nicholas Robinson, who were both concerned about seeking better protection for Dublin's historic buildings and more positive action to protect them. Kevin Nowlan was an Associate of Modern History in the National University of Ireland and Chairman of the Dublin Civic Group and the Dublin Architectural Study Group; Nicholas Robinson was a solicitor and chairman of the National Trust Archive, the recently established photographic record of buildings in Ireland. The special challenges they faced deserved a wider audience and the perfect opportunity presented itself in March 1980 in Brussels – a major conference on preservation organized by Europa Nostra. The editor of *Country Life* agreed to publish a special report for distribution at the conference, *Dublin's Future: the European Challenge*, written by Kevin Nowlan, Nick Robinson and Alistair Rowan – my predecessor at *Country Life* but by then Professor of History of Art in the National University of Ireland.

While discussing the report with them on a second visit I spent an afternoon in the Library of the Irish Society of Antiquaries looking through eighteenth- and early nineteenth-century books for visitors' impressions of the city. Almost all were struck in equal measure by its beauty and by the poverty. John Barrow in his *Tour round Ireland* (1836) observed: "Of all the cities which I have seen, not Petersburgh even excepted, Dublin displays every species of patchwork in its buildings and its inhabitants, more in extreme and more in juxtaposition, than any other I believe in the world – splendid equipages mixed up with filthy hackney-coaches, elegantly dressed ladies jostled by half-naked beggars – noble streets with houses like palaces hemmed in by dirty lanes and wretched hovels." John Carr in his *Stranger in Ireland* in 1806 wrote: "Dame Street is the great focus of fashion, bustle, business and is lined with noble shops and buildings. It is the Rue St Honoré of Paris and the Bond Street of London: and the beauty of the principal streets of Dublin is not disfigured as in London by an intermixture of butchers' fish-mongers' and poulterers' stalls, which are confined to certain quarters of the town." Many visitors admired Dublin's wide streets. To Anne Plumptree, in her *Narrative of a Residence in Ireland* (1817), Portland Place in London, Sackville Street in Dublin, and the Canebière in Marseilles " . . . were the three widest streets I have any where seen," while St Stephen's Green was larger than "any square in London".

Today many of the grander houses in and around Merrion Square and St Stephen's Green have been taken over as offices – often by Government Boards of various kinds. These Boards have not gained the bad name that so-called Quangos have in Britain, and walking round these squares and streets and seeing the nameplates of different boards outside each building, it is difficult not to feel, their establishment in former houses opening directly onto the street gives Government in Dublin a more human face than in countries where all official activities are concentrated in huge

ministries which the public rarely approach.

The first problem identified by Kevin Nowlan and Nicholas Robinson was lack of protection. While in Edinburgh, for example, 2541 buildings and groups of buildings were then statutorily listed. The Dublin authorities, in their current review of the draft development plan, recognized only 399 buildings and groups in the city as worthy of preservation, and in no case was the value of an interior considered. Under the 1976 Planning Act a planning authority could indicate the preservation of interiors as a planning objective, and require owners to obtain permission for their alteration or removal – in Waterford some interiors were in fact protected in this way. But in Dublin the City Surveyor had advised against such protection because of the overall time and cost involved.

OPPOSITE: A mid-18th-century panelled room in 13 Henrietta Street, Dublin. Despite long neglect the interior survived remarkably unscathed. ABOVE: Houses on the west side of Parnell Square in Dublin: each house differs subtly from its neighbour in colour and design.

CARBURTON STREET TRIANGLE

The outlook of the simpler Georgian terrace house in London was, for all the protection of listing and conservation areas, rather worse than in Dublin. Early in 1981 three particular cases were worrying us at SAVE, each involving not just a group of Georgian houses, or even a street, but a whole block.

The worst of these three cases was the so-called Carburton Street triangle, just south of Euston Road and west of Fitzroy

Square. The houses under threat lay along Carburton Street and
Great Tichfield Street, with two further houses in Greenwell Street.
Externally, like so many Georgian houses in Dublin, they were
plain though well-proportioned, mostly with stuccoed ground
floors and three storeys above, finished with a parapet. What they
had also in common with many Dublin streets was that they were
not built as uniform terraces but in groups of two or three by local
masons and joiners. These were not what was officially rated the
first class of London houses in the eighteenth century (usually
designed by architects), but evidence of the kind of building local
Georgian craftsmen produced, working on their own account. I
learnt something of their history from a report the Community
Housing Association prepared by Anthony Richardson and Partners
examining the potential for rehabilitation.

192, Great Titchfield Street had been contracted for by James
Hagley who undertook to build with "good substantial materials
. . . good even coloured malmstock bricks . . . joysts rafters purlins
doorcases and window cases to be all of good yellow fir the sills to
be of good oak". James Hagley had died before building began and
in 1791 his widow sold the rights of the agreement to Thomas Piper,
a builder and surveyor of Ogle Street. The houses were completed
in 1794. The plots in Greenwell Street, the future numbers 5–7 were
taken by a local builder, William Doncom. Number 6 became the
home of John Flaxman, the great neo-classical sculptor, who lived
there from 1800–26, and altered the house about 1810. Numbers
184–190 Great Titchfield Street and 26–27 Carburton Street were
built by two local carpenters John and James Reid between 1791 and
1794. The rest of the Carburton Street houses were built by William
Richardson, another builder and carpenter, between 1808 and 1811.
He was the son of George Richardson whose *Book of Ceilings*, first
published in 1770 was widely used by plasterers all over Britain.
George Richardson had worked for eighteen years in the office of
Robert and James Adam and the book was of great importance in
popularizing the Adam Style. William Richardson's interiors contained decoration reflecting current fashions – notably reeded
plaster strips and rosettes on and around chimneypieces, doors and
windows.

The houses had been included in Westminster's Slum Clearance

Programme in 1970, but had been listed by the Department of the Environment in September 1974. The Council had decided none-theless to proceed with compulsory purchase and clearance, and a public inquiry was held in June 1977. This proved something of a fiasco as, just days before it was held, the Greater London Council's Historic Buildings Division had withdrawn its evidence on the history and architecture of the buildings. This was transparently a political decision taken by the new ruling Conservative group at County Hall elected in May, who wished to prevent the submission of evidence which might obstruct proposals put forward by fellow Conservatives at Westminster. As the GLC's Historic Buildings Division always prepares its case with immense thoroughness, no-one else had wanted to duplicate its work. With no evidence on the merits of the buildings the inspector agreed with Westminister's witness, and concluded the architectural interest of the buildings was "slight". They were not representative, he concluded, of the best London domestic architecture of the period and "although the houses form terraces, the terraces themselves are not units of design". But by this last argument most of Georgian Dublin could be demolished. The inspector embarked on another curious line of reasoning for demolition: the Georgian buildings were not con-sistent with modern buildings nearby.

This was in July 1978; with a new Government the next year a renewed campaign was mounted to save the houses. Antony Richardson's proposals provided accommodation for a range of different sizes of families which, in total, would have housed 70 people compared to 76 in the Council scheme. The cost of new building, was, he calculated, one third more than rehabilitation. A new reason was now adduced for demolishing. Following con-firmation of the compulsory purchase order the Council was legally obliged to demolish the houses. In an attempt to encourage councils to have second thoughts on clearance schemes, the 1974 Housing Act had relieved local authorities of this duty to demolish but only in cases where the compulsory purchase order was made before 1975 and the Carburton Street triangle order had been confirmed in 1978.

And so the Carburton Street triangle was demolished. The real tragedy is that the process is now continuing across the rest of

Fitzrovia. While the Georgian houses in and around Charlotte Street seem safe, those south of Euston Road are likely to go, street by street. Yet these terrace houses, often no more than two or three windows wide, with shops below, give character and variety to the area. Where there are doors to houses, shops and restaurants every six or seven yards along a street, people are constantly coming and going. However, when these buildings are replaced, particularly if they are rebuilt as offices, there will often be only one entrance in a whole section of a street. The result is a gradual death of street life. Where there are shops and small offices above, people are constantly mingling and pausing in the street when they meet. This was expressed most vividly by a planning officer from Lewes District Council while Max Hanna and I were preparing a report *Preserve and Prosper* published in 1983.

Such continuing, needless destruction of usable housing is dispiriting indeed, but on 31 May 1984 a counterblast of the most rousing kind came from a very unexpected quarter. The Prince of Wales, addressing a gala evening organised by the Royal Institute of British Architects at Hampton Court, made a swinging attack on the treatment of Britian's towns and cities. "At last people are beginning to see that it is possible, and important too in human terms, to respect old buildings, street plans and traditional scales . . . At last, after witnessing the wholesale destruction of Georgian and Victorian housing in most cities, people have begun to realise that it is possible to restore old buildings and, what is more, that there are architects willing to undertake such projects."

"For far too long," the Prince said, "some planners and architects have consistently ignored the feelings and wishes of the mass of ordinary people in this country". And remembering the line of policemen that stood guard while St Agnes Place in Lambeth was demolished against vigorous protest from local people, it is interesting to note that the politician who referred lovingly and proudly to "His Majesty the Pickaxe" as he smashed his way through the streets leading up to St Peters in Rome was none other than Benito Mussolini.

OPPOSITE: Late Georgian houses in the Carburton Street triangle in Westminster, London. A scheme had been drawn up by a housing association for their repair but was rejected and the houses have been demolished.

INDUSTRIAL BUILDINGS

"YOUR OWN PICTURES SHOW that these are ghastly warehouses where only a few parts have any architectural merit – even Sing-Sing and Alcatraz were better designed. I think you will make yourself a laughing stock if you ask people to help you save these frightful and ugly buildings." Such was the tirade we received at SAVE in December 1978 from a leading property developer who had made a speciality of conservation. The attack was in response to our campaign to save the great group of East India Company warehouses in Cutler Street, on the edge of the City. About half of the buildings were to be wholly demolished; the remainder were to be gutted and to lose their little-touched interiors. The champions of the Cutler Street warehouses were no less fierce or eloquent. Sir James Richards, author of the Penguin *Introduction to Modern Architecture* wrote: "The Cutler Street Warehouses are among the noblest specimens remaining and could be preserved and still serve modern needs. It should be unthinkable to destroy even one of them." The architect Fello Atkinson concurred: "If they were in Venice or Chicago instead of London the world would cry out for their preservation." Mark Girouard described the great zig-zag Middlesex Street front of the warehouses as "one of the grandest pieces of street scenery in London".

These diametrically opposed perceptions of just one group of buildings highlight the particular dilemmas and problems of seeking to preserve industrial buildings – people can have a hostile mental image of the buildings which can not only close their eyes to any architectural quality they may have but make them aggressively

OPPOSITE: Randolph Langenbach's view of the Colne Valley near Scaithwaite in West Yorkshire. In the foreground are pre-Industrial Revolution weavers' cottages, below is Titanic Mill dating from 1912.

determined to see them destroyed. Of course, empty decaying industrial buildings can seem overpoweringly depressing because of their sheer size. But by the same token when they are rescued and reused they are inspiring to an equal degree. This journey is therefore one of troughs and peaks – of great abandoned buildings now lifeless and decayed, contrasted with others, once equally forlorn, but now teeming with life and activity. For me it began, not with warehouses or mills but railway architecture.

RAILWAY ARCHITECTURE

In the autumn of 1976 SAVE set to work preparing an exhibition on railway buildings including not just stations but engine sheds, railway hotels, vaiducts, bridges and whole railway villages.

Just before Christmas in 1976, I went to see the head of British Rail's public relations department in the hope of hearing some official words of wisdom on the subject. They were indeed blunt. "Historic Railway Buildings," he expostulated. "We'd knock the lot down tomorrow if only someone would give us some money to replace them." Immediately we had a masthead for our exhibition. For these few words perfectly enshrined an attitude towards historic buildings found throughout the public sector. They are seen as a burden, a continuing drain on resources because of the maintenance involved. Yet, in the same breath, money is expected, large sums of money, for their replacement. With British Rail, this abandonment of ordinary maintenance is visible on station canopies the length of the country. Again and again we heard the argument: "Our first priority is our track, our second the rolling stock, stations are third and with all the cuts we're facing, and with our engineers crying out for funds for track and rolling stock, how can you expect us to spend money on luxuries like historic buildings." At first, the logic sounds inexorable, but it contains a fatal flaw. Any organization in the private sector would be keenly concerned about the face it presents to the world and spend money to ensure that the first impression it gives to the public is a good one. Offer railway passengers a questionnaire as to where they would like to see changes – cleaner trains, cheaper fares, more frequent services – and they will certainly put these before restoring stations, but that can never do away with the vital psychological role of the station in giving the passenger his first impression of what rail travel will be like. While London's Victoria Station was being steadily cut to pieces, it was fascinating to see streamlined the facade of the Victoria Coach Station (built in 1931–32 to the designs of Wallis Gilbert & Partners, architects of Firestone and numerous other crack 1920s factories) being handsomely refurbished as offices for the National Express Bus Company.

Just how a well-restored station can become a focal point of city life was brought home to me in Zurich. The *Hauptbahnhof* is a massive classical building looking across to the River Limmat which flows through the city into the lake. In recent years it has been cleaned and restored with the zeal and care usually lavished on opera houses in great cities – the ceilings of the arcade along the front have been picked out in Victorian colour schemes while inside the station is filled with shops and restaurants and cafes of different kinds. There are no barriers preventing free access, made unnecessary by that great Swiss institution, the ticket collector on every train. Most fascinating of all, on a Sunday afternoon, when London stations would be torpid if not empty, was to find that every restaurant and cafe was overflowing with people enjoying a Sunday outing. The beer hall was full of old age pensioners with brimming jars of beer; the cakehouse packed with children devouring immense icecreams and sundaes; the restaurant still crowded with customers gently digesting their enormous lunches while cigar smoke spiralled up into the high Victorian ceilings.

Nothing could be a starker contrast to the life and glamour of Zurich Station than the railway station at Derby. In June 1982, I went to Derby to see the much praised restoration of the railway cottages there by the Derbyshire Historic Buildings Preservation Trust. The photographs I had seen of them before restoration had made them seem dreary as only rather fuzzy black and white photographs of derelict buildings can, so the contrast on arrival was all the more startling. The railway cottages are laid out on a triangular pattern: they are very plain but well-proportioned – their appeal comes principally from the lovely, unexpectedly soft pink

ABOVE: The railway station at Derby. Despite vigorous opposition British Rail pressed ahead with demolition in 1984.

brick of which they are built. I arrived just as a shower was brewing. The cottages were in sharp sunlight but the sky behind was a steely grey and I could never have seen them at a better moment. The vivid pink and grey were those of Moroni's brilliant portrait *Il Cavaliere in Rosa* – one of the high points of the Royal Academy's *Genius of Venice* exhibition in the winter of 1983–84. As I hurried round taking photographs, I began to notice all the other railway buildings nearby, railway warehouses, railway institute, the Midland Hotel and the Station itself with a long *porte cochère* flanked by three-storey pavilions – an unusual, indeed, noble composition.

Derby Station was under threat and almost twelve months later to the day I returned, this time by rail. It is hard to imagine a more depressing sight than the station platforms at Derby – and although built after the war they give off that bomb-site feeling of utter desolation and neglect such as still remains in the centre of East Berlin. As I stepped down from the train, the tannoy boomed out to my surprise: "Would Mr. Binney of *Country Life* please come to the Assistant Station Master's Office." I found the Assistant Station Master, complete with an information sheet on the station. After a tour of the platforms, we entered the station building itself. Long as the platform was – it was no preparation for the size of the station buildings. Walking round was a nightmarish version of the tour of discovery in *The Leopard* made by Tancredi and Angelica round the abandoned apartments of Don Fabrizio's palace at Donnafugata. A railway station in such circumstances can never have the glamour of a country house: at Derby it was not simply the occasional cobweb, but broken glass, rubbish strewn everywhere, pathetic dead birds, the steady drip of water. But as we walked round a magic did emerge for here, sealed in behind locked doors, was a building that told the whole history of the rise and decline of a great railway company. Very little, I thought, had survived of the original 1840 station described in *The Gem of the Peak* (1843) as "the most complete and magnificent Station yet erected". This was sad as the original station was the work of Francis Thompson, architect of the fine stations at Chester and Cambridge and numerous delightful smaller country stations. Yet buried within later additions the Greek Revival detail began to emerge – chimneypieces, sash windows, panelling, doors, balustrades. The whole building was a palimpsest of railway architecture – one layer laid over another.

History came alive in the great boardroom of the old Midland Railway. The boxes for the rollmaps of the railway network survived along the wall: we peered out through the massive plate glass sash windows – the largest sash windows I have ever seen. From here we filed through, like generations of Board members, to arrive on a platform in the great shareholders' room, high above the main floor of the room where the assembled shareholders sat to hear news of the company's fortunes.

Emerging into the sunlight, the significance of the station as a reflection of change and growth rather than of a perfectly preserved architectural statement of one period, became apparent. The original station was contemporary with Brunel's Temple Meads. The shareholders' room was added in 1857, the board room in 1872 – in London club palazzo style. The *porte cochère* was built between 1852 and 1857 by John Holloway Saunders, the Midland Railway architect, but moved forward to its present position by his successor Charles Trubshaw. But for all its history Derby Station was condemned. British Rail had drawn up plans for a replacement and the funds were available.

The case for preservation was twofold. First the Derbyshire Historic Buildings Preservation Trust, fresh from its triumph with the fifty-seven railway cottages, all repaired and resold, had offered to take on all surplus parts of the railway station, repair them and find users or purchasers for them. British Rail could thus spend its funds on rehabilitating those parts of the station which it needed and be freed of responsibility for those it did not. Second, the station is the focal point of a railway village, comparable only to that at Swindon. Immediately opposite is the Midland Hotel, also designed by Francis Thompson, which opened in 1841. The railway cottages were built in 1841–42. The Brunswick Inn forming the point at the end of the triangle also opened in 1842. Across the tracks is the huge Derby Railway Works, parts of which are listed, while opposite the cottages are a large group of railway warehouses. All these buildings are in varying shades of red brick and as the cleaning of the railway cottages shows, this brick when cleaned looks very handsome.

"There are good reasons to be angry about Derby Station," I wrote in *Country Life* on 8 September 1983. "Angry first, with British Rail for determining to press ahead with demolition and rebuilding even though no detailed study has been made of the cost and practability of repairing the existing station . . . Angry, secondly, with the Department of the Environment for steadfastly refusing to list a station which still vividly reflects the growth and development of one of the great Victorian Railway Companies. Angry, thirdly, with Derby City Council for granting permission to demolish the focal point of the Railway Conservation Area it designated in March 1980."

Meanwhile opposition to British Rail's proposals was mounting. Sir Peter Parker, the outgoing Chairman of British Rail, was bombarded with letters asking for a change of heart. "We have no intention," he replied, "of following a policy of demolishing or making major alterations to good historic buildings when it can be demonstrated that the old buildings can be properly and sympathetically conserved to the benefit of the business." But British Rail would only discuss the re-use of surplus parts of the station if their reconstruction proposals did not go ahead.

On this occasion British Rail's intransigence was to pay off. The twelve-month reprieve did not materialize and the bulldozers came on site in April 1984. Derby Railway village which could have been the earliest and most complete railway settlement in the world has lost the building which was its *raison d'être*.

TEMPLE MEADS

The treatment of railway buildings like Derby Station is to me tragic. It is also ironic because there are few, if any, organizations with more enthusiasts for the history of their own industry than British Rail. Just how positive and helpful this enthusiasm can be I know from serving as Chairman of the Brunel Engineering Centre Trust which has taken on the task of restoring Brunel's original station at Temple Meads in Bristol. Opened in 1840 this has the distinction of being the oldest railway terminus in the world – not the oldest railway station I hasten to add as Liverpool Road in Manchester being restored by another trust, has that laurel.

Pugin, in his *Apology for the Revival of Christian Architecture* published in 1843, wrote savagely about Brunel's Temple Meads and its companions: "The Great Western Stations are mere caricatures of pointed design, mock castellated work, huge tracery . . . ugly mouldings, no meaning projections . . . make up a design at once costly, and offensive, and full of pretensions." In fact, cost much more than show had been in the minds of the Bristol Committee in approving Brunel's Tudor Gothic design. On 27 July 1839 the Secretary of the Bristol Committee, Thomas Osler, had

ABOVE: The front of Brunel's Great Western railway terminal at Bristol. The station is now being restored.

written to his London colleague that Brunel was instructed to prepare plans for offices "which were to be as devoid of ornament as was consistent with decent sightliness". Brunel's first scheme, Osler said, was Tudor. "The second, with the exception of an open arch or gateway of the simplest kind at each end – consisted I think of as thoroughly naked an assemblage of walls and windows as could well be permitted to enclose any Union Poor House in the country." To their surprise the Directors had found "the cost of the 'Tudor' front would exceed that of its Quaker companion by just £90!" The Tudor style was therefore chosen partly for the further reason that it: "harmonized with the bridges and archways already built west of Bath, and with the better specimens of Bristol architecture generally."

A letter in Brunel's letterbook in the Public Records Office, dated 10 September 1839, explained the ground floor contained: "rooms sufficient for a good residence for the head clerk, while the

ABOVE: Brunel's hammerbeam roof trainshed at Temple Meads, Bristol.

board room, secretary's room and waiting rooms" were on the first floor, with a general office above.

The most spectacular part of Brunel's train design was the great hammerbeam roof trainshed. Such a broad roof, with a depressed or flattened arch would normally produce a strong outward thrust, but as the station was raised on arches it was impractical to counter such a thrust in the normal way by the use of buttresses.

Brunel's grandson in his *Life of I.K. Brunel* (1870) explains the method adopted: "There are no cross tie-rods but each principal of the roof is formed of two frameworks, like cranes meeting in the middle of the roof; the weight being carried down on columns near the edge of the platform, and the tail ends of the frames held down by the side walls. As the two frames do not press against each other at their meeting point at the ridge of the roof, there is no outward thrust."

Brunel himself provided some further details at a meeting of the Institution of Civil Engineers in 1849. The roof was " . . . formed by framing timber together, plating them on both sides with iron, and disguising the construction by ornaments applied to the timbers, instead of working them in the timber. . . . The style of architecture to which it has been applied, particularly demanded bold mouldings which could, by this system, be worked on the edges of the bent timber, in the direction of the grain, and the strength of the wood was never impaired." Brunel made this comment, interestingly, in a discussion about the roof of East Horsley Park in Surrey where the hall roof introduced by Lord Lovelace in 1847 had trusses bent by steam. Brunel thoroughly approved the new system – an example of a country house being at the forefront of developments in technology.

The hammerbeam roof shed was the passenger terminus proper, but between this and the office block was an inner shed, more utilitarian in design, with a flat roof, resting on cast iron columns where other operations took place. Here Brunel devised an ingenious hydraulic travelling frame to lift coaches from one track to another. This was described by his Assistant, Arthur John Dodron, to the Institution of Civil Engineers in 1844. The purpose was to move the carriages from the arrival side to the departure side, without resorting to a turntable. A cast iron frame was lowered across the track and the carriage placed over it. By means of a large pump acting on hydraulic presses at the corners, the frame was raised till it touched the axles of the carriage wheels. A smaller pump was worked to lift the flanges of the wheels from the rails; next "the whole apparatus, with the carriage suspended upon it, is then easily transported to any of the lines of rails" and then lowered, "the whole transit not having occupied more than a minute and a half".

The cost of the frame which was made by A. Napier was just £220, and Brunel added, at the end of the meeting, that it was the first of its kind.

The Bristol lines had opened on 31 August 1840, with the terminus still unfinished and "the last rail not well and truly laid more than half an hour" before the first train left shortly after 8 a.m. But when I first saw Temple Meads it was in a very desultory state. Brunel's trainshed was a car park, the office building was empty and gathering dust, the drawing offices over the inner train shed were deserted and beginning to leak.

The initiative for the Brunel Trust came principally from Tim Organ of Form Structures and Tony Byrne, then working at the Ironbridge Gorge Museum, who became Secretary of the Trust and has been its prime mover ever since. Form Structures had produced a scheme for establishing a trust to take on Brunel's terminus and had begun negotiations with the Western Region of British Rail's property board. British Rail had recently had its own survey of work needed on the building producing a grand total of £2 million. This was daunting enough, but equally so was the problem of finding an appropriate use. The obvious use, a Live Steam Railway Museum, with steam engines puffing out of the trainshed onto the main line as well as stationary exhibits was ruled out: British Rail had built a signal box, controlling the whole regional network, across the mouth of the train shed, leaving no space for a line to come in or out. Traffic problems were even more of a headache. British Rail understandably did not want a use, or a form of access which would increase the number of cars arriving at the station. As the busiest single stretch of road in the whole country of Avon passed immediately in front of Temple Meads the local authorities shared their concern.

The future Trustees were therefore faced with complex negotiations with both British Rail and the planning authorities. We wanted a simple enabling planning permission for change of use to a range of cultural and associated activities but as Temple Meads is a Grade I listed building we had to submit detailed plans, not outline ones for approval. The principal means of reducing British Rail's figure of £2 million for restoration was to use labour financed by the Manpower Services Commission. In the final negotiations for the lease we were exceptionally lucky in securing a new trustee. The Vice-Chairman of the trust, Bob Thornton was Chairman of Debenhams and had suggested his colleague John Roberts who concluded the negotiations with astonishing vigour, and has since taken on the direction of the trust's working committee.

Brunel's terminus was a daunting building to acquire in such circumstances – the only comparable rescue, of Manchester's Liverpool Road station, had massive support from the County Council prompted by the 150th anniversary celebrations in 1980. When a building has been empty and disused for some considerable time and many bright ideas for its future have come to nothing, local people can become sceptical about yet another proposal and it takes time to build up confidence. At Temple Meads the trust's work has progressed slowly but steadily. British Rail had re-roofed the office building just before the trust signed the lease on 29 September 1981. The trust has cleaned, cleared and decorated the offices and the arches below so they are ready for use: the appearance of the trainshed has been transformed. A start has been made on the external stonework, parts of which were savagely eroded and decayed.

By the beginning of 1984 the Trust had raised and spent more than £1 million on the repair and restoration of the Brunel's Terminus. A Youth Training Scheme with 45 training places for 16-year-old school-leavers was in operation, with up to 13 staff to supervise them. At the same time the Trust was operating a Community Programme, designed for long-term unemployed adults (aged 19 and over) with approval for 36 participants. With such schemes the numbers employed vary constantly as recruits come and go but the Trust had been averaging up to 80 per cent full capacity. More gratifying still, of 29 trainees who left in the six months following September 1983, 25 had gone to full-time jobs.

The great moment with any long empty building such as this comes when at last it is thronged once more with people. At Temple Meads we achieved this at a great gala evening and banquet on Saturday 11 June, 1983, brilliantly organized and stage-managed by Tony Byrne and John Roberts. No less than 1200 people came – all in 1930s dress. Brunel's trainshed became an enormous dance floor – with the platforms on either side serving as galleries to watch the dancing, and a great sunray motif behind the band at the end. The inner, columned part of the trainshed was filled, end to end, with trestle tables – yet even then there was not enough room to sit.

The gala evening commemorated the 150th Anniversary of the Bristol Committee of the Great Western Railway. Tony Byrne had organized the event to coincide with the last day of the Bath Festival and half the guests were to come from Bath in a special train drawn by the locomotive King George V, one of only two remaining King Class locomotives. Designed by G. B. Collett it had been introduced by the Great Western Railway in 1927. The 13 Pullman coaches behind it were of 1960 date, but repainted in the Great Western Railway's chocolate and cream livery. The Bristol guests also arrived by train – partly because British Rail did not want the station forecourt choked with cars by people attending the gala. This train was drawn by LMS locomotive 5000, built at Crewe in 1935, and designed by Stanier. She was one of just 18 of the 842 of her class to survive. As the train made the short journey from Wapping Wharf to Temple Meads it was staggering to see hundreds and hundreds of people lining the track, or looking out of windows and waving – if so many people will turn out to see one steam-drawn train the Trust must have a great potential in Brunel's terminus for all the problems and challenges it presents.

The locomotives met face to face in the modern station. Hundreds of figures in blazers, white ducks and boaters streamed onto the platform.

MILLS

The SAVE exhibition *Off the Rails* generated a vast amount of public interest. Given the love people have of steam engines and railway history, this is not surprising. What we did not expect was that SAVE's second exhibition on industrial buildings, namely the textile mills of Yorkshire and Lancashire would strike an even stronger chord.

This was a journey that began in the summer of 1977 late one afternoon when I was tidying up paperwork after the Victoria and Albert Churches Exhibition *Change and Decay* had opened. There was a knock on the door and a tall wiry American who had been studying at the Institute of Advanced Architectural Studies in York arrived to show me a dissertation he had just completed on textile mills. To Randolph Langenbach, a New England photographer, designer and writer, textile mills, I soon discovered, were life and blood itself. What he had brought me was a photocopy of his dissertation. There are times when photocopies of photographs produce an image even stronger than the original. The blacks become blacker, and the highlights whiter, producing an image almost like an etching. Photocopies in particular give strength and presence to humble buildings like simple terrace houses, where every detail of brickwork can stand out with startling sharpness. The austere architecture of the mills and chimneys in Randolph's photographs, set against the dramatic backcloth of the Pennines, had a grandeur and majesty I have never imagined. I was so taken with these images that I promptly showed them to Michael Darby, then the Exhibitions Office, at the Victoria and Albert Museum, as the subject for a future exhibition. But the Victoria and Albert had other things in mind and mills became a SAVE venture. The title of the exhibition chose itself, Blake's famous 'Dark Satanic Mills' in the hymn *Jerusalem*, and early that autumn I set off in search of textile mills with Ken Powell, a Victorian Society activist living in Leeds, as my guide. I little knew this particular journey would lead in two years to the establishment of a northern office of SAVE with Ken Powell as secretary.

Photographs can exaggerate or raise expectations unduly, but Randolph's pictures, despite their deliberate drama and intensity, in no way put a gloss or veneer on the buildings. The sheer intoxicating quality of the Pennine millscape is for me best captured in Ronald Willis's *Yorkshire's Historic Buildings*.

For all its faults it is Europe's most romantic industrial landscape. A well-known film director taken to a hill above Halifax said simply "It's too much". In other words, so perfectly "West Riding" that the uninitiated would have difficulty in accepting the scene as anything but a grossly heightened version of reality.

Industrial buildings such as mills may be grand and impressive, they may be handsome, but relatively few are what most people would call beautiful. I think they are best described as sublime. They have precisely the qualities that Edmund Burke, the great eighteenth century philosopher and statesman, describes in his *Essay on the Sublime and Beautiful*, published in 1756: Obscurity, Power, Privations, Vastness, Infinity, Succession and Uniformity, all qualities which combine to induce a sense of awe, and ultimately of terror in the onlooker. For Burke, the Sublime stands to the Beautiful as a stormy mountain landscape by Salvator Rosa does to a tranquil sunset by Claude Lorraine. On analysis the textile mills embody these qualities of the Sublime in just the same way that a great Palladian house set in rolling parkland epitomises Burke's conception of the Beautiful. They impress first of all by their scale. Four, five or six storeys high, twenty or thirty windows long, they inevitably induce a sense of awe by their sheer size. (Burke considered height the most moving kind of vastness.) This effect is increased by their starkness – sheer walls punctuated only by uniform rows of windows. From behind the massive stone walls often no light emerges – the Vacuity, Darkness, Solitude and Silence that Burke saw as Privations. Often it is only the smoke from the chimney which signals a mill is at work (Burke's Obscurity) except on winter evenings when the lights are visible.

Undoubtedly the mills in the Pennines gain much from their setting, the sudden twists in the valley bottoms and the increasing barrenness of the hills as one climbs – small stone-walled fields gradually giving way to open moor. What is hard to imagine is just how many mills there are – or were – for today they are disappearing at an ever increasing rate. They stand in clusters in the valley bottoms, hugging the rivers that were essential to the steam engines that drove them. They stand in open country in pastoral settings surrounded by fields and reflected in the waters of large reservoirs. In landscape terms, they have an added appeal because they are often seen in sequence or in groups – even the plainest mill can become part of a visually arresting composition simply by virtue of the way it is seen with its neighbours. At their grandest they are ambitious and sophisticated in architectural terms, not just solidly-built and well-proportioned, but rich in detail and silhouette.

The earliest mills tend to be plain, the only architectural flourish being a Venetian or Diocletian window in the end gable. One which stands out in my mind is Woodhouse Mill, near Tod-morden. I first saw this one Sunday morning in October 1982 driving up over the Pennines from Hebden Bridge to Brooksbottom on the Lancashire side. The countryside here is spectacular, a broad canal winding along the valley, the hills rising sharply on either side with the walls and trees giving way to moorland. Suddenly the mass of Woodhouse Mill came into view standing in elegant isolation on the far side of the canal. The walls rise sheer from the water, their blackened stone contrasting with the vivid green of the fields around. The mill is of classical proportions with what looked at a distance to be row upon row of Georgian sash windows, surmounted unexpectedly by a pediment. We crossed the river to find to our surprise that the mill was open and there were signs that repair was under way. There was no sound of anyone, so after calling out we began slowly to ascend the staircase when suddenly came the pounding of footsteps descending anxiously or angrily from several floors above. Thirty seconds later the new owner was before us, suspicious, but not hostile. We learnt that he had just acquired the mill and was making it a home for his collections of machinery and equipment rescued principally from other textile mills as they were demolished. The mill was not listed and only a few weeks before he had been negotiating with the previous owner to buy, knowing there was a demolition contractor with cheque book ready in the next room, keen to acquire it simply for the scrap value of the building materials.

This is an abiding problem with textile mills. There is a major demand in West Yorkshire for recycled stone, partly because planning authorities often insist that extensions, and even new houses, are built of local stone. In addition, the massive timbers used in mills to support the machinery are much in demand as large seasoned timbers of this kind are virtually impossible to find today. As a result a demolition contractor can make a profit out of demolishing a mill, regardless of whether he sells the site.

In December 1978 I drove over the Pennines with Ken Powell to look at mills in Lancashire. The snow was falling steadily and we did not see the great mill at Bacup until it was immediately in front of us. It was, I remember, a stupendous sight, dominated by a massive tower that gave it an almost Byzantine appearance. The tower looked some 15 storeys high, perhaps an illusion caused by the small

ABOVE: Ross Mill at Bacup, Lancashire, during demolition in 1982. A huge and magnificent Edwardian cotton-spinning mill of red brick and terracotta, which had been in full use with modern machinery only three years before.

OVERLEAF: View over Milnsbridge near Huddersfield in Autumn 1977. In the Colne Valley the whole industrial landscape – mills, chimneys, weaving sheds and viaducts – survives.

windows that studded the walls, and the upper stages took the form of a polygonal turret continuing the vertical thrust of the buttresses which ran up the sides of the tower. It was a remarkable experience on that bitter morning, having seen in the previous months so many empty mills, to go inside and find the whole mill humming with the sound of machinery. We ascended from floor to floor, six in all; each was brightly lit, with modern looms operating at capacity. The whole building was in excellent condition and it was difficult at that moment to imagine a mill could be more secure. Yet three years later came devastating news – Ross Mill at Bacup had closed; all the machinery had been taken out and the building acquired by a demolition contractor.

I wrote to Tom King, Minister of State at the Department of the Environment, who I had been to see a little while before to talk about incentives to re-use industrial buildings. If Ross Mill was to be saved it had to be listed and here the problem was its date, Edwardian. Ross Mill was not deemed to be of sufficient special interest to be added to the statutory list. This was in January 1982, and a few weeks later Bacup lost its major landmark. But the poignancy of the loss was well captured by Ian Beazley who photographed the mill when only the tower was left standing. At that moment it still rose to the height of the factory chimney, towering above the demolition cranes below.

Architecturally, the most spectacular of the Yorkshire Mills is undoubtedly the Manningham Mills complex in Bradford. This was built to the design of the famous Bradford partnership of Lockwood and Mawson, who were responsible for many of the best Victorian buildings in Bradford including the soaring Gothic town hall (later brilliantly extended by Norman Shaw). If the town hall deliberately recalls those of medieval Italy, such as Sienna with its great tower, so Manningham Mills, consisting of two parallel ranges without a centrepiece, reminds one of the Uffizi in Florence. The Italian analogy is completed by the extraordinary chimney – square in plan and modelled on Venetian campanile – like that in St Mark's Square. It is given added richness with an upper stage above the main bracketed cornice: it is said the directors had dinner at the top of the chimney in a hastily contrived dining chamber when it was completed in 1873. Manningham Mills are all the more a landmark since they have been cleaned on the initiative of Bradford Corporation during Operation Eyesore in the early 1970s. When I went round them in 1977 they were completely empty as they remain to this day. The company, Lister's, had concentrated all its machinery in the lower ranges of weavers' sheds at the back and everything taken out of the twin ranges. Even when they are empty, mills look impressive for they are almost always constructed on an open plan so an entire floor can be seen at a glance – always through a vista of the cast iron columns that supported the weight of the machinery.

What can one do with vast empty buildings such as these? My first reaction was that they would make a spectacular home for the

Indian Collections of the Victoria and Albert Museum. Bradford, it is true, has no particular historic connections with India or the East India Company as, say, Liverpool has, but it has a large population of Indian and Pakistan origin. At the time the Indian collections of the Victoria and Albert Museum were sitting almost in their entirety in store. They had been displaced from the grand series of rooms in which they were housed when Imperial College was extended in the 1950s and successive Governments had failed to fulfil their promise to rehouse them. I wrote to Roy Strong suggesting that the Victoria and Albert Museum Indian collections might go to Bradford as an outstation of the museum. He responded with interest but alas the Department of Education and Science promptly quashed the idea as his Museum was then negotiating for another building in London. Little did I know that at virtually the same moment, from across Exhibition Road, the Science Museum was planning to open a National Museum of Photography at Bradford.

The sheer scale of textile mills at first seems overwhelming when it comes to the question of reuse. But inspiration comes once again from America, principally from the great mill towns in New England. The scale of the mills in Massachusetts and New Hampshire is phenomenal. Compared to the Yorkshire mills some are as a Buick is to a Volkswagen 'Beetle' or a Mini.

My first introduction to the great mills of America was Lowell in Massachusetts, a town famous for its "mile of mills" along the Merrimack river. Lowell was the first of the New England mill towns. In 1820, the population was just 200; by 1836 there were eight major textile companies with nearly 7,000 employees. Lowell boasted the largest cotton mill, the largest woollen mill and the largest carpet factory in the United States. By 1850, Lowell was the second largest city in Massachusetts after Boston. In the 1920s the New England textile industry collapsed even more dramatically than in Lancashire and Yorkshire. Lowell lost virtually all the early housing built for the mills but the canal system, which had been central to the city's growth, survived largely intact as well as seven out of the ten great mill complexes in the town.

When I first went to Lowell in October 1978, Congress had just voted forty million dollars to create a National Industrial Park in the town – the urban counterpart of the great National Parks which

contain some of North America's most spectacular scenery. It was an extraordinary project, virtually unthinkable in Britain in spite of all the years of talk about regenerating the inner city. At that moment there was very little to show for it, apart from a smart visitor centre, although the mills standing silent and empty were a majestic sight. All these mills were of red brick rather than stone, five, six or even seven storeys high, many of them reflected memorably in the canals immediately below. Three years I found had made a remarkable transformation: most of the buildings in the central downtown area had been cleaned and painted. Work was under way on an enormous group of mills which were being converted into apartments. Other mills were to be converted to a variety of uses – shopping, offices and exhibition space. In rediscovering its past the city had gained self-confidence.

From Lowell, I went on to Peabody just north of Boston, bordering with the historic town of Salem famous for its great houses – which featured to such advantage in the film of *The Europeans*. At Peabody there was a converted tannery I particularly wanted to see. I arrived in a perfect late afternoon light. The name, The Tannery, was painted in large brown letters around the base of the chimney near the entrance; the development company had originally intended to name it Crowninshield Estates but it soon transpired that most of the potential purchasers were people who had actually worked in the tannery. Externally the building was plain, with virtually no ornamental detail of any kind, yet the strength of the colour of the brickwork, combined with the huge buttresses supporting one of the fronts made it extraordinarily imposing.

These American success stories gave us hope on which to build. What we had never expected was the intensity of public response when 'Satanic Mills' opened. Within ten days, the first printing of the companion book to the exhibition had sold out. This was almost entirely through orders by post from people living in Yorkshire and Lancashire. Usually at least half of the orders we receive at SAVE come in neatly typed and franked envelopes from business addresses

OPPOSITE: Manningham Mills, Bradford completed in 1873 to the designs of Andrews and Pepper. It is now largely disused.

but almost all of these were from home addresses from people to whom the mills were a major element in their lives. In preparing the exhibition we had feared the satanic image of the mills would count against them – the memories of long hours, bad working conditions, low wages, pollution and industrial disease, would make people want to see them disappear from the landscape. In fact the strength of local interest and feeling was astonishing and ironically the strongest expression that mills should be erased from the landscape came in a letter to *Country Life* written from Kent, in response to an article I wrote on mills in January 1978.

I wonder if I am alone [David Tomlinson wrote] in thinking that these enormous mills are nothing more than huge and ugly blots on the landscape; sad and decaying reminders of a ruthless industrial period when the erection of such buildings was allowed to go unchecked, ruining many a fine landscape. Now that these mills have long outlived their period of usefulness and stand gaunt and derelict it is surely time to get rid of them. Mr Binney says that "many mills are in park-like pastoral settings"; how nice it would be if the emphasis in these park-like settings could be returned to the pastoral, and the disfiguring mills completely removed.

However, despite all the intense response we received the great mills of the Pennines are disappearing at an ever increasing rate. Here and there an enterprising individual, or entrepreneur or local group acquires a mill and restores it, but local authorities lack the resources and the will to take determined action. Ministers and officials at the Department of the Environment consistently refused to help us in the search for new uses. We formulated a plan to carry out a series of studies suggesting practical and viable new uses for redundant mills, as we had done with Billingsgate Fish Market and were doing with Battersea Power Station. I was invited to a meeting at the Historic Buildings Council. One Department of the Environment official showed considerable interest in the proposal, and as he clearly managed a budget of considerable size my hopes began to rise. "This is certainly an interesting and worthwhile idea," he said. "But we only support research which takes at least two years and you are proposing to do this in one. So it won't qualify. And anyway all our available funds are likely to be absorbed in granting extensions on research already commissioned." I was dumbfounded but I looked round the room at the officials present and clearly not one of them saw anything unusual or curious in the remark. I left fuming that such a total lack of urgency or concern could exist. Yet as I write I have just learnt one piece of good news stemming directly from *Satanic Mills*. Randolph Langenbach has been appointed Professor of Architecture at Berkeley in California – one of conservation's most perceptive and eloquent champions will open the eyes of a new generation to the sublime grandeur of textile mills on both sides of the Atlantic.

BATTERSEA POWER STATION

The same passionate feelings, both for and against, are evoked most strongly by another great industrial building: Battersea Power Station. I became involved in August 1978 when 'Nationwide' ran a piece that Battersea Power Station was to close in three years time. I was invited to comment on the news. The interviewer told me a story which stands for quite a number of people's view of Battersea Power Station: he had been driving a Glaswegian friend over Chelsea Bridge and pointed to the Power Station saying, there's one of London's great architectural monuments. There was a long silence until his companion replied "Ye're taking the piss."

I have long been an admirer of Battersea Power Station and living just across the river I always saw its soaring white chimneys and great plumes of smoke twisting in the sky. The best view of all was at night from the Embankment on the north side of the Thames where every evening the great river front was floodlit. The lighting brilliantly picked out the architectural detail, especially the soaring vertical ribs which thrust up towards the chimneys. Battersea Power Station is not beautiful: to me it is one of the best examples of the most exciting architectural style the twentieth century has produced – Expressionism.

Expressionism is principally associated with the name of Eric Mendelsohn, a German architect whose powerful drawings portray a vision of a sculptural architecture of streamlined curves and dramatic silhouettes. Battersea Power Station, in the vigour of its modelling, is sculptural, but more than this it is brilliantly expressive of its purpose. In the nineteenth century so many new building types were disguised – often to superb effect – in the trappings of the public buildings of their day. Sir Giles Gilbert Scott, architect of Liverpool's Anglican Cathedral, might have done just this at Battersea as he was called in to make the initial design more acceptable to the public. He was, it seems, unhappy about the upturned table effect of the chimneys, when he became involved in 1930, but this could not be changed. Instead, he chose to make a virtue of it, emphasising the vertical lines at the corners, and the bases of the chimneys are stepped inwards so the whole building becomes visually a pedestal for the great cream smoke stacks. As a result there is no mistaking Battersea's purpose; it forcefully and unmistakeably proclaims its role to every passer-by.

Our first problem however, was to gain a closer look. I had never been nearer than the train which hurtles past over Grosvenor Bridge into Victoria Station. Initially, we met with a rebuff, so we wrote to Tony Benn, then Minister of Energy, explaining our interest in seeking alternative uses, and suddenly all doors opened, and on a clear but grey January day in 1979 we were met by the Director-General of the South-East Region of the CEGB, and an impressive posse of officials and engineers and given the grand tour. Having donned freshly laundered white overalls and bright yellow safety helmets, we were taken into the great turbine hall of Battersea A station. Without question this was the largest hall I had ever entered, 500 feet long, 100 feet wide and 120 feet high. We had entered at ground level and the noise that greeted our ears was overpowering. The noise was not that of turbines, but of pneumatic drills and demolition machinery – Battersea A, we learnt, was being stripped out. This was a tragedy, and may yet prove to be the act which doomed the building. The Historic Buildings Council, I later learnt, had recommended the Power Station for listing in 1978, but DOE officials had decided to suppress the recommendation in case it interfered with the Electricity's Board's plans for the site. The turbines were being stripped out for their value as scrap – though for all the value of the special metals, we heard, it covered little more than the cost of demolition. So there was no financial gain in this wrecking operation.

The turbines had stood on huge piers and were linked to the sides of the hall by a system of bridges and galleries, with large open wells looking down to the floor below. All these galleries, and the numerous staircases leading down to ground level had marvellous key pattern balustrades and stainless steel handrails. All were now being taken out – though the railings, we were told, would be stored. Here was a great Egyptian Hall, lined on either side with towering square pillars, clad in tiles. In treatment it was like two versions of the Hoover Factory facing each other across a street, and the steel girder acting as an entablature had a purpose: carrying two massive gantries which cruised up and down the length of the hall, built to move heavy parts needed for the turbines. Now it seems they were being used in a more sinister way, as the tools of the hall's destruction.

When the turbine hall was still in use and every surface glistened, it must have been a stunning sight – it is tragic that it was never properly photographed in colour when in its prime, though such photographs may get emerge. From here we went to the control room. This, like the turbine hall, was the work of the original architects of the power station, the Manchester firm of Halliday & Agate. Here the walls were panelled with marble and the ceiling was worthy of a jazz age grand hotel or ocean liner. All the control equipment was still in place, and in one corner on a table was a splendid scale model of the Power Station.

We went up to the roof and saw the chimneys closer to. The geometrical brickwork of the towers was almost Aztec in its elaboration. Here, too, was evidence of one of Battersea's problems – as an air pollution control measure, cooling chambers had been constructed at the bottom of the chimneys to extract certain gases, and some of these gases had worked out sideways through the brickwork. Repointing was urgently needed but as the brickwork was only a cladding to the steel frame, it was not, we gathered an insuperable structural dilemma.

The problem we now faced was how to proceed with finding a new use. First, there was the problem of sheer size. Second, Battersea was not in such an advantageous position commercially as Billingsgate Market. Offices, the use which would generate the highest rents, even if it was practical, would be resisted by Wandsworth Council. Our first need was for an architect to draw up a scheme and David Pearce, one of SAVE's founders, suggested Martin Richardson, who had been sharing his office with Chrysalis,

the architects of SAVE's Billingsgate Scheme. Martin Richardson's first problem was to obtain plans of the building. The CEGB professed to have none, only charts showing the layout of power cables. But by ingenious means he procured a set of the original plans, something the CEGB to this day do not appear to have. On 14 October 1980 came the news that Battersea Power Station had been listed by Michael Heseltine. Now the CEGB were bound to look seriously at its future. A few days later *The Times* diary jokingly offered a prize of £10 to the reader with the most practical solution for its future. The response was overwhelming. As *The Times* diarist wrote on 27 November: "One thing is certain, Londoners love Battersea Power Station."

Martin Richardson and I began to talk to developers: it became clear that the size of the building meant there would have to be a mix of uses. One plus was that two storeys of car parking was potentially available within the building, enough for 1300 cars beneath the main operational level. The solution we proposed in a report, *The Colossus of Battersea* published in 1981, was for a giant indoor sports arena within the main block. Martin Richardson showed that the arena would conform with the standards of the European Athletics Association, providing seating for 8000 around a four-lane 160-metre running track. Alternatively, it could seat 10,000 if used for indoor tennis. At the time both the Sports Council and the GLC were looking for a site for a major indoor arena and willing to spend a substantial sum. Soon after the South-Eastern Region of the Sports Council produced a report advocating sports use in Battersea Power Station, but in the event both withdrew. Wandsworth's planners, however, told Martin Richardson they had found his scheme inspirational and granted permission for change of use on the lines we suggested.

The purpose of the report had been principally to cast bread on the waters – and after a year we had two positive responses. First the Lesser group of companies had drawn up a scheme for making Battersea Power Station a rubbish incinerating plant which they were convinced could operate in competitive terms with existing

OPPOSITE: The Turbine Hall of Battersea. OVERLEAF: London's Battersea Power Station from across the Thames on a winter afternoon.

means of rubbish disposal. The second reponse, more intriguingly, came from an accountant who had drawn up plans to make the Power Station into a giant dinner-dance theatre like the Lido in Paris. His theory was that such shows could only work with a really large audience and required a very big building seating up to 2000 people – far larger than any conventional theatre. Trying to get planning permission for a new building for such an activity would, he thought, be an impossible struggle – but within an existing building such as the Power Station it would work.

On 18 October, 1983, the Central Electricity Generating Board launched the Battersea Power Station Competition, aimed, according to the Prospectus, " . . . at finding a use or uses which will ensure the future of this massive structure." A panel of assessors had been appointed with Lord Ezra, former Chairman of the National Coal Board, as Chairman. The competition was in two stages. Applicants had to register by 9 January 1984 and submit entries by 5 March (these dates were later extended to 20 January and 19 March respectively after pressure from applicants for more time). To register an applicant had to be of "suitable financial standing and ability". This meant a well-established development company. Martin Richardson began writing letters but every time drew a blank. Friday 20 January passed and we had still found no developer. The next week Martin Richardson suddenly heard from a large practice of architects he had contacted – hours before the closing time for registration – that they had found a major property company with leisure connections, and put in an entry.

At three o'clock the next Thursday I arrived at a large meeting in the architects' offices. The conference room was packed: the developer, architects, engineers, surveyors and quantity surveyors – a full professional team. There was an immense sense of purpose and direction. A package of uses would be quickly worked out, the cost of repairs and conversion assessed and potential revenue from tenants calculated. The scheme was to be a mixture of retail and leisure – whether it would be an up-market Brent Cross-type shopping mall or a drive-in Do-it-Yourself supermarket was not yet clear. At this meeting I was given a copy of the CEGB's "Answers to Questions" dated 5 December 1983. One of the principal questions, I was amused to read, was what planning permission existed for the site. And the CEGB had to answer, just one: permission for change of use from Wandsworth Council for leisure and recreation purposes granted to Martin Richardson on behalf of SAVE Britain's Heritage on 29 April, 1982.

However, when I returned to the same room about a fortnight later all our hopes were dashed. The engineers considered the cost of repairs would be much higher than originally envisaged. The leisure uses would pay their way once established but the whole initial cost of installation would have to be met from other sources. The total forecast for revenue from retail was less than £1 million per annum. "If the Electricity Board wish us to preserve the building as part of the nation's heritage," said the Chairman of the meeting, "they'll have to give us at least £10 million." I sighed and smiled. For one thing was certain, the CEGB would never pay a penny towards the preservation of the building. Our chance was lost, and worse, for all the figures were to be submitted to the Competition Office and thus provide the CEGB with an added argument for demolition.

There were still, as far as I knew, ten other competitors: two I knew were keen and committed enough to continue – the question was would the others all withdraw? Suddenly a few days later I received a call from a financier SAVE had once helped at a public inquiry, trying to prevent demolition of a listed barn he had wanted to restore. The inspector had supported us, but the Minister, for reasons we could never fully divine, had overturned his inspector's recommendation. But this time the news was good. "I have a fantastic scheme for Battersea Power Station," he told me. "Will you join the team?" A few days later I found myself in the conference room of a large firm of chartered accountants in the City, watching a high-powered presentation of the scheme. Once again the key question was finance; would the merchant bankers advising deem it a worthwhile investment. On Friday 16 March, three days before the closing date for entries, came the long awaited news – the bankers had produced a letter saying "Yes" the scheme was fine and they would raise the £40 million required.

The CEGB put the seven competition entries on show in Battersea Arts Centre on 4 April. I had to go to Nottingham that day, and could not attend the press view. The report in *The Times* the next day suggested the CEGB were hardly overflowing with

ABOVE: New Concordia Wharf overlooking St Saviour's Dock on the South Bank of the Thames, half a mile to the east of London's Tower Bridge. Restoration as apartments is nearing completion in April 1984.

enthusiasm at the entries. "We were not consulted on the listing," Mr. Geoffrey Stone, regional director of the CEGB was quoted as saying. "We would have been happier if it had not been listed." Further on he was quoted as saying: "If there is a nil result from this competition it will have been reasonably demonstrated that there is no commercially viable scheme for this building." I blinked as I read this: how could there be a 'nil result' when there were seven finalists all of whom had been through the stringent financial hoops set by the CEGB. That morning I went along to the exhibition. To my delight it was milling with people and the competition entries were indeed bold, varied and exciting. One of them, of course, was the one I was supporting but as I write I am still bound by the rules of the competition to anonymity. The schemes included, in the competitors' own words, London's first leisure and entertainment complex of world standing; a major conference centre; a mix of high quality flats, hotel, retail and covered mall; and a 2600 seat theatre restaurant capable to staging 'Busby Berkeley' scale shows.

My colleague, Clive Aslet of *Country Life* was more enthusiastic than *The Times*. "I thought it was marvellous. Some of the schemes were really imaginative." The result of the competition will be announced by the time this book is published. To some, trying to preserve Battersea Power Station will seem, as I was once told by an elegant lady who had just restored a Cornish farmhouse, "sheer perversion – perverted preservation". But to me it remains the greatest of all historic building challenges – the Mount Everest of Preservation.

WAREHOUSES

"Decision time for the Thames" proclaimed the cover of *The Sunday Times* colour supplement on 19 April 1981 in bold red letters over a photograph of Michael Heseltine with the charred shell of a Victorian warehouse behind him. Mr Heseltine, the article ran, "depending on what decisions he takes on the schemes he has before him now . . . can sign a blank cheque for a further spread of the blight of concrete filing cabinets which already spoil so much of the Thames – or open up the possibility of an exciting renaissance for the run-down acres of riverside dereliction that have been festering since the war". But just months later Michael Heseltine was to condemn the very warehouse he had been portrayed against, overturning his inspectors' recommendation that it should be retained. His action doomed one of the most evocative areas of warehouses left in London.

The saga of London's riverside wharfs and warehouses in the last ten years is perhaps the saddest story there is to tell in this book, and the fact that there are any success stories at all is due to the enterprise of a few determined individuals.

The warehouse Michael Heseltine had condemned had the unusual name of St Mary Overy's Wharf, which it took from a priory that once stood just beside Southwark Cathedral. It was founded, the legend runs, by the daughter of an avaricious ferryman, who used her father's fortune to endow the priory.

Here it was not just one warehouse that was at stake but a

ABOVE: The ornate front of St Mary Overy's Wharf in Southwark, London.

remarkable area around Clink Street, which took its name from the Bishop of Winchester's ancient palace, a fragment of which survived there. The Bishop had a damp underground prison, hence the expression "the clink".

When *Country Life* moved to the south bank, the Clink was the nearest area of real atmosphere and character to our new offices. However, it was rapidly becoming a battleground. The warehouses were being bought by developers. New Hibernia Wharf on the north side of Southwark Cathedral had been sold for £850,000 in 1977, just as a plan to rehabilitate it, and create a square in front of the cathedral, was on the point of receiving planning permission. The new owners, Bernard Sunley Investment Trust put in a second application to redevelop the site which was waiting consideration when fire destroyed the building on 30 November 1978. St Mary Overy's Wharf now stood guard at the eastern end of the area, and this too had been badly burnt. Clive Aslet writing in *Country Life* on 3 January 1980, described it as: "perhaps the most ostentatious warehouse along the Thames. . . . It rises five storeys in a once gay patchwork of red, yellow and blue brickwork, sandstone facings and terracotta ornament, so strikingly pretentious that it caused something of a scandal when it was built in 1882."

The area to the west of St Mary Overy's Wharf was a remarkable survival – isolated by the railway from Cannon Street which sweeps round on arches in a great curve towards London Bridge Station. Along Clink Street the cliffs of warehouses survived on both sides connected by iron bridges high above the street. Everywhere the area had a sense of enclosure because the narrow streets followed the medieval pattern: here you could completely forget the endless thunder and vibration of the stream of heavy lorries accelerating along Stamford Street and Southwark High Street. Clink Street turned into Winchester Street, still cobbled, surrounded by warehouses but just large enough to be a remarkable suntrap, completely sheltered from the wind. Had it survived just another ten years every warehouse would no doubt have been repaired and converted. Alas this area was caught in the tail end of the great property schemes of the Sixties and Seventies when the efforts of property companies were concentrated on assembling large sites. The acquisition of sites along the river was a process which inevitably took time, and was further extended by prolonged confrontations with the planning authorities during which warehouses were just left to rot.

The tragedy had begun at St Katharine's Dock, next to the Tower of London. In 1979 Taylor Woodrow had won the contract for the dock on the basis of a scheme which would retain the majestic warehouses around the dock. These had been built to the designs of the great engineer Thomas Telford (1757–1834). Telford was the son of a shepherd, but had been apprenticed to a mason, and after working on Edinburgh New Town had become County Surveyor of Shropshire in 1788. Five years later he had been appointed Surveyor to the Ellesmere Canal and turned his activities entirely to engineering. The St Katharine's Dock warehouses, begun in 1825, were the first in England to be designed so ships could berth alongside and unload directly into the warehouses – before goods had always been landed on a quay. As a result the great blocks of warehouses had the formality of a magnificent Georgian square. But Telford's 'A' warehouse was spectacularly burnt for a film about the Blitz, while consent was given in 1974 for the demolition of warehouse 'C' on the understanding that 'B' was to be retained. However, in 1976 Taylor Woodrow had produced a report with a brontosaurus on the cover explaining that 'B' warehouse also had to be demolished.

The story of the saga of St Katharine's Dock has been well told in E.R. Chamberlain's *Preserving the Past* (1979) but it is worth quoting from the preface of Taylor Woodrow's report: "The Late Chairman Mao Tse-Tung," it begins, "advised 'we should make the old serve the new' a challenge to every conservationist and to all who have a sense of history. But sometimes the old can't be made to serve the new. However interesting a brontosaurus, it is not the sort of creature one can turn into a house pet." Taylor Woodrow wanted to replace 'B' warehouse with a building of equivalent size, forming an extension of the world trade centre. I arrived one Sunday morning to see the cranes hard at work demolishing the remains of Telford's 'B' warehouse and I watched the destruction of the great columns he had placed along the water-front. As warehouses were utilitarian buildings he had used the simplest and most primitive of the classical orders – massive unfluted Doric columns with a very pronounced entasis – or swelling – towards the bottom. They were cyclopean in feeling like the great buildings above. 'C' warehouse in fact outlived 'B' and survived longer until early in 1981 I arrived to see this too awaiting imminent demolition.

Today St Katharine's Dock has a new colour of life from the mass of boats which are moored there, and 'B' warehouse has been rebuilt to a design intended to echo its predecessor. But to the old building it stands as a modern reproduction table does to a Georgian original. The new warehouse is faced in a warm plum-coloured brick that completely changes its character – for all its size it has none, in my view, of the grit and presence of Telford's building. The Ivory House, built later than Telford's, cleaned and restored in the centre of the dock stands as testimony to the grandeur the dock might have had.

Hard after St Katharine's Dock came the loss of the battle over the Cutler Street warehouses, described at the beginning of this chapter. This was followed, in turn, by permission to demolish the

ABOVE: Lobby of the Admiral Hotel in Copenhagen.

five great blocks of the London Docks, begun in 1804 to the designs of Daniel Asher Alexander.

Permission was granted to demolish the London Docks without even an inquiry – there was a proposal for a major printing works, creating jobs, which no minister was likely to oppose. But the London Dock area was a huge site, much of it already cleared, and no consideration was given to retaining some of the warehouses while building alongside.

Just how well great dockside warehouses could be adapted to new uses I learnt on a visit to Copenhagen in 1980. Here on the waterfront was the Admiral, a large new 366-bedroom hotel installed in an eighteenth-century Granary. This was a building of heroic proportions, built in 1787 of much the same white brick as the London Dock warehouses but now brilliantly clean. The hotel brochure proudly proclaims the historical events it has witnessed: "the battle of Copenhagen of 1801 which was fought practically outside its windows. And six years later, the merciless bombardment of Copenhagen by the British.''

Walking into the hotel lobby it was astonishing to find all the massive eighteenth-century timbers still in place. The huge Pomeranian pine beams in fact had been preserved throughout the building not only in the hall but in every bedroom. ''Most modern hotels are without any distinctive character,'' the brochure continued proudly, ''but not the Copenhagen Admiral, which is a scheduled building.'' To add interest one end of the lobby contained a fascinating display of model ships on loan from the Royal Danish Naval Museum.

It was not just the Copenhagen Admiral which had been restored so spectacularly, but a whole line of warehouses running nearly half a mile along the waterfront, all dating from the late eighteenth century and built just in front of the Royal Palace of the Amalienborg. These had all been converted into apartments, and I later learnt the story of their rescue from the architect Hans Munk Hansen, who had been responsible for the long warehouse in the centre known as the Yellow Warehouse, from its bright yellow paint. These warehouses, he said, had been designed by the Court architect C.F. Harsdorff, for a merchant, Frederic de Conick, who had built them as an exchange for exotic goods from East Asia, Africa, and the Danish West Indian islands. The Yellow Warehouse had subsequently become a customs warehouse in 1898, but seventy years later had been gutted by fire. ''Fortunately, even in this condition,'' Mr Hansen continued, ''the building was listed under the Protection of Buildings Act, so the authorities stood out against plans of pulling down the ruin.'' Plans for a museum fell through, but then a residential scheme was drawn up which if not ''as much in accordance with the original use'' helped solve another problem – the depopulation of the Amalienborg quarter, which was becoming increasingly dead after office hours. The conversion was carried out by a Co-operative Society – like an English housing association, formed by the individuals who later occupied the flats. These future owners guaranteed the bank loan which provided the finance for the work. The Yellow Warehouse has three entrance halls running through the building from one front to the other and the flats open off a central core on each floor. All 35 flats run from front to back, so each has a view of the harbour. As the warehouse was on a very deep plan, the flats were given living rooms of generous proportions – 35 square metres, with a dining-kitchen and two bathrooms in the centre of the building. Rubbish chutes, box rooms and a shared laundry – all the extras of a modern apartment block – had been provided. The principal external change had been to the windows which were too small to meet daylighting requirements and had been widened by five inches on each side. In the hotel, however, even the original window apertures had been left intact.

What was interesting, with these warehouses, was that each had been restored and converted in a different way, retaining more or less of the original features. Externally the most successful of all was the Nyhavn hotel, where the brownish brickwork had a wonderful patina and modern balconies very sensitively created in the original loading bays on the upper floors. The interior of the Nyhavn, unlike the Admiral, was entirely new, though the restaurant had large wooden beams in warehouse style – such was the desire to create a warehouse atmosphere. The Nyhavn was one of a group of hotels owned and run by a family, and such was its success that they were even interested in acquiring a warehouse as a hotel in London.

One of the sons came to London to look at the possibilities and I took him straight to Shad Thames, among the most atmospheric streets in the whole of London. It runs east from the foot of Tower Bridge, on the south bank. Here you step back into the world of Dickens – great cliffs of warehouses rise on either side and the street is criss-crossed by bridges and galleries at every level – like one of Piranesi's famous *Carceri*. Just by Tower Bridge was Courage's Anchor Brewery which had recently closed – at the east end, Shad Thames turned at right angles and ran south beside a long broad creek – St Saviour's Dock – once the outlet of the River Neckinger. The Neckinger sounds like a river flowing through Germany into the Baltic and appropriately the warehouses along St Saviour's Dock which among London's great riverside wharfs survive intact, have the look of a creek in some distant Hanseatic port. We arrived that day at high tide, the best time to see St Saviour's Dock. Gliding out of the murky waters of the creek was a family of swans, glistening white against the soot-encrusted fronts of the warehouses.

When I returned three years later on 12 April, 1984, the whole scene was transformed, and this time at last the news was good. The largest of the warehouses, New Concordia Wharf, was transformed – the London stock brick cleaned and now a brilliant almost buttery yellow, all the decaying ironwork newly painted in royal blue. New Concordia had been acquired by a brilliant young entrepreneur, Andrew Wadsworth who at one point had helped us with Battersea Power Station, setting his quantity surveyors to work on a costing of Martin Richardson's scheme.

New Concordia was being transformed into flats, 60 in all, with 20 industrial units, a restaurant and underground car parking. New Concordia was built in 1885, the year the foundations were laid for Tower Bridge, as a series of grain warehouses. The builder, Seth Taylor, was a rich grain merchant who named the warehouses after Concordia near Kansas City, from where much of the grain was imported.

By April 1984 many of the flats were already occupied and the success of the project was assured. The architects, Pollard Thomas Edwards and Associates, had been at pains to retain every existing feature but where new work had to be introduced – such as stair-cases and galleries – they had taken the detail from ships and yachts they had studied in St Katharine's Dock just across the river. New balconies and railings had the characteristic ball joints and tele-scoped balisters of ships' steps. All the windows had been replaced in steel following the original pattern of thick glazing bars with rosettes at intervals – the only change was to make them into casements – the originals had been the characteristic tip windows found through docklands. Inside the original cruciform cast iron columns had been kept throughout the building as well as all the floor timbers. Fire regulations had been met by putting a very thick coating of concrete on each floor leaving the splendid timbers exposed on the ceiling below. Local sign writers had been brought in to paint the numbers on all the doors in traditional style.

The flats varied very much in size and were selling from £38,000 to £180,000. The really stunning part was the views on every side – across St Saviour's Dock, north, over the Thames, west to Tower Bridge and down river to Rotherhithe. Climbing from floor to floor, the views became more and more spectacular; the climax came at the top of the water tower, now a studio-penthouse lit by great arched windows on all sides. Andrew Wadsworth's office immediately below was equally unusual – an old customs craft previously at Thames Pier, and now permanently moored like a pier head in the river, rising and falling with the tide.

FIRESTONE

The grimmest journey I have made to look at an endangered building brought me, soon after quarter past nine on the morning of Bank Holiday Monday on 25 August 1980, to the Firestone Factory on the old Great West Road in Hounslow. I had arrived back from a holiday in Switzerland late the night before and opened the Sunday paper to see a report that demolition had begun that Saturday morning. A quick telephone call to David Atwell confirmed they had been working all weekend to wreck the building.

I arrived at the climax. It was a beautiful morning and two large cranes from St Mary's Demolition Company were gouging out the great centrepiece of the factory. It was an extraordinary sight, the building was being attacked relentlessly as if in a medieval siege: the cranes were swinging great balls back and forth to crush and destroy every single architectural feature. As I arrived, the upper parts of the remaining giant pillars were receiving a final battering and they collapsed dramatically before my eyes, leaving nothing but a great wound in the centre of the building. In front, a group of figures watched casually, some reclining comfortably on the grass. On the pavement outside the gates a cluster of local people looked on helpless or bemused. What was so extraordinary was that it was only the centre of the building which was attacked, the long low wings were perfectly intact and indeed were to remain so for months.

There was no doubt in many people's minds that this was a preemptive strike to prevent the buildings being listed, and subsequent newspaper articles confirmed that the Department of the Environment would have spotlisted the factory the next day. Trafalgar House, the developers who were acquiring the site from Firestone, were quoted as saying: "We just moved in as part of the normal development procedure," and "The weather was right for it. In our climate you must do that sort of thing when you can." The story was soon about, however, that when people working in the offices behind the facade had gone home on Friday evening, they had no idea they would return on Tuesday to find their offices no longer existed. The food store for the canteen, we heard, had come under attack, and joyful demolition men had gone home clutching large hams and haunches of beef. How many of the stories were true I do not know, but the simple fact was that not only had Firestone been destroyed but the focal point had been torn from one of the most remarkable groups of industrial buildings in the whole of Britain. Harold Clunn had captured the spirit of this industrial arcadia in his *London Marches On* (1946) "West of Syon Lane the ultra modern factories standing back amidst green lawns . . . look so ornate, that they might easily be mistaken for the mansions of merchant princes and potentates of some great city in the East."

More than any other group of buildings in London, they had made a deep impression on me as a child. I remember them at night when the facades were floodlit, and especially at Christmas when the great Firestone front was lined with Christmas trees and decorations. These were the products of the age of the streamlined look, immensely colourful and stylish, bringing to life great names familiar from advertisements. The marvel of it was that here was a whole area, consistently laid out as a grand processional way.

Not all the buildings were as good as Firestone, but they were all in the same mould. The factories continued for the best part of a mile, beginning with Beecham's, now hidden beneath the M4 flyover, and concluded with the great tower of the Gillette Factory. The Firestone factory in particular was always so well kept, the facade so brilliantly white, the lawns so perfectly mown, that no-one appeared prouder of it than its owners. Yet in the middle of July 1980 I had gone with Clive Aslet to look at these factories with a view to suggesting they should be protected by listing or the designation of a conservation area. On our arrival, there on the gate was a planning notice announcing an application to redevelop the Firestone Building. On our return Clive Aslet telephoned the Hounslow Planning Office only to be told the application had been withdrawn. We both wrote separately requesting the listing of the factory. However, weeks elapsed and Firestone was destroyed just before the building was listed. The real tragedy was that Firestone was architecturally no more than a showpiece facade; it would have been perfectly possible to demolish the large factory behind and make this into industrial units, as Trafalgar House proposed, retaining only a line of offices at the front.

The original architect of Firestone, Thomas Wallis, had made a speciality of factories – the Hoover Factory on Western Avenue being his other best known work. His philosophy had been expressed in a speech of 1933 to the Royal Institute of British Architects: "The industrial architect should, without extravagance, endeavour to give a pleasing effect to his facades, relying as far as possible upon the necessary planning and layout for good and proportionate lines. He could go further and say that a little money wisely spent in the incorporation of some form of decoration, especially colour, was not money wasted. It had a psychological effect on the worker . . . A little money spent on something to focus the attention of the public was not wasted money, but was good advertisement."

Our fury was intense. Simon Jenkins, the vice-chairman of the Thirties Society was quoted as saying: "The loss of the factory is a disaster. It was one of the top two or three buildings of its kind in Britain."

Incensed, I wrote to *The Guardian* describing the destruction of Firestone as "the most brutish and despicable act of calculated vandalism I have ever seen". Today my verdict remains unchanged. "Can a company," I wrote a few days later in the *Evening News*, "that owns the Daily Express, whose Fleet Street office is one of the acknowledged showpieces of the period and which owns Cunard (the Queen Mary was *the* great art deco monument) really be excused?" We attacked the Department of the Environment for its reluctance to list buildings of the 1920s and 1930s. Here we struck a chord. Michael Heseltine was also furious with Trafalgar House. On 14 October he announced the listing of some 50 buildings of the interwar period. One of these was Battersea Power Station. And that battle, as we have seen, continues.

OVERLEAF ABOVE: The Firestone factory in July 1980. The best of the great series of inter-war factories along the old Great West Road in Hounslow, London, and a high point of Art Deco in Britain. BELOW: An orgy of destruction: the Firestone factory crashes to the ground at 9.30 a.m. on 25 August 1980.

CONCLUSION

"Conservation is a comparatively new idea," Michael Manser, President of the Royal Institute of British Architects, claimed in the *Financial Times* on 11 January 1984. The best answer to this is a Roman inscription recorded in James Russell's *Letters from a Young Painter Abroad to his Friends in England (1750)*. He quotes a decree condemning demolition as "the most cruel kind of traffic in Herculaneum". "If any person for the sake of traffic [ie profit] should have purchased any building, in hopes of gaining more by pulling it down, than the sum for which he bought it, that he shall be obliged to pay into the exchequer double the sum for which he purchased it". This was written before AD63 when Herculaneum and Pompeii were engulfed in lava from Vesuvius.

What is relatively new is people's confidence to stand up and speak out for endangered buildings. There have always been some people willing to do this, but today there are many. Yet the idea that there is somehow a silent majority against preservation dies hard. The old-fashioned view was put by an MP of long experience to the Parliamentary Committee investigating the Land Fund in 1977. "If what remains of our heritage is to be saved," he wrote, "it must be saved not by publicity but by stealth." His reasoning was that whenever economies were being sought, the Arts and Heritage were always Target No. 1.

The purpose of this book has been to show that these fears can be cast aside. Fine buildings can be saved if people are willing to speak out for them. The response can be remarkably swift. In the middle of October 1983 virtually no-one in Britain had heard of Calke Abbey. Ten weeks later its fate had become a national issue. The announcement that Calke would be saved came in the Chancellor's budget speech on 13 March 1984. That same speech also brought devastating news – Value Added Tax was to be applied to major rescue operations on historic buildings of all kinds – from Barlaston to Battersea Power Station – a 15 per cent levy which would cripple the economics of such projects. SAVE had to fight back.

"You haven't a cat's chance in hell," one colleague told me sanguinely. But weeks later we had won. However to tell that story and the continuing battles waged over policy issues, as well as individual buildings, would require another book.

INDEX